GRACE BEFORE MEALS

GRACE BEFORE MEALS

FOOD RITUAL AND BODY DISCIPLINE IN CONVENT CULTURE

PATRICIA CURRAN

UNIVERSITY OF ILLINOIS PRESS
Urbana and Chicago

Publication of this work was supported in part by a grant
from the Andrew W. Mellon Foundation.

This book is printed on acid-free paper.

Library of Congress Cataloging-in-Publication Data

Curran, Patricia, 1940–
    Grace before meals : food ritual and body discipline in convent
culture / Patricia Curran.
        p.   cm.
    Bibliography: p.
    Includes index.
    ISBN 0-252-01585-1 (alk. paper)
    1. Monastic and religious life of women.   2. Sisters of Notre Dame
de Namur—Massachusetts—Customs and practices.   3. Dominican
Sisters of Mission San Jose—Customs and practices.   4. Food habits—
Massachusetts.   5. Food habits—California.   I. Title.
BX4210.C87   1989
255'.97204—dc 19   88-34851
                                                            CIP

CONTENTS

PREFACE

This work was made possible by the fortuitous confluence of a number of factors. First of all, it was my good fortune to have lived with an international community of religious women from various congregations in a Dominican convent in Berkeley, California. It was there at supper table one evening that the conversation turned to the silent meals of our past. Those of us who had been members for twenty years or more were startled to discover that though the formality of our ritual past was similar, the rituals themselves differed significantly. Some never spoke to one another in the dining room, not even at Christmas or Easter. Others spoke on occasion but ate while on their knees. These sisters also changed their places at table regularly, having no discernible order to the ranking of the members. Yet others sat in a fixed hierarchical order that was so powerful that when a sister died, a candle was lit at her empty plate for thirty days; only then did the next in age move up to fill the vacant space.

Some of these religious families took root in another millennium, yet an unbroken chain of celibate mothers and daughters had handed down their way of life from generation to generation, preserving what was held sacred in the past into our own time. A series of parallel cultures had existed, each maintaining secrecy about the nature of its corporate discipline.

Having interests in religious dance, theology, and anthropology, I was intrigued by the richness of the topic. I wanted to hear and understand what the dining customs were saying about food and body, about movement and stillness, about sanctity and sin. I wanted to record what the practitioners had to say about their participation and its effects, to record their private interpretations as I explored symbolic meanings.

This book is an extension of that table conversation. In the process of writing it I discovered much more than I originally wanted to know. For all who assisted in expanding the parameters of my vision, I am deeply grateful. At the top of the list stand William Cieslak, OFM, Cap., professor of liturgy at the Graduate Theological Union, and Nancy Scheper-Hughes of the Anthropology Department of the University of California, Berkeley. This list includes those who came aboard after the first draft was written, the anonymous readers who critiqued that effort for the University of Illinois Press.

My special thanks go to the superior of the convent where I lived, S. Allyn Ayres, OP, who happened to have been stationed at her motherhouse in 1963, the year I chose for a thick description of one convent meal. Whereas I relied on my memory for details of movement, space, and gesture in Notre Dame, I relied chiefly on hers for the Dominicans. Her patient and gracious responses to a daily barrage of questions allowed me to write the opening chapter.

It was my good fortune to have been generously assisted by archivists who spent many hours preparing for my visits to their California sites. I am indebted to the late Sr. Mary Justine McMullen, SND, of Belmont, who died suddenly during the final phase of our collaboration; to Sr. Mary Paul Mehegan, OP, of Mission San Jose, who both located and translated the founder's letters from the original German; and to Rev. Leo Cullen, SJ, of Los Gatos, whom I saw but once, but will remember for his hospitality and humor and for sharing anecdotes from his own novitiate training, which made all those documents stamped "For Ours Only" come alive.

I have been deeply touched by the generosity and simplicity of the more than fifty women who gave me access to their lives in formal interviews. I hope they find themselves in this completed work and appreciate, as I do, the value of their contribution.

The last fortuitous circumstance is my membership in the Boston Province of the Sisters of Notre Dame de Namur. They are the women who commissioned me to study, who allowed me to determine the shape of those studies, and who, despite their severe financial constraints, underwrote my costs. This volume is my gift in return. May it illuminate our future as well as our past.

INTRODUCTION AND GLOSSARY

The food rituals of the Dominican Sisters of Mission San Jose and of the Sisters of Notre Dame de Namur are the subject of this study. Their dining place, the refectory, is a ritual arena where the sisters portray their understanding of discipleship; using gesture, posture, movement, silence, and speech to give thanks to God for all that sustains them—food and faith, life and grace—and to renew their commitment to follow Christ, despite their unworthiness and imperfection.

In this ritual arena nature and grace are competing forces, therefore food has an ambivalent status. It is valued as a gift of God necessary for human life, but it is also feared as a potential source of sensate pleasure capable of disrupting the inner focus on spiritual realities and therefore endangering the pursuit of perfection.

I demonstrate that in the course of the twentieth century a common understanding and acceptance of the rituals gave way to private interpretations, to rejection of perceived meanings, and to inner resistance to their public performance. By 1960 the rituals lost their power to transform, to bridge the ever widening gap between the sisters' personal values derived from the secular culture and those embedded in the religious culture.

Those with authority to govern, however, considered these rituals to be a sacred part of their inheritance and continued to teach them to new members even when they themselves resisted the messages encoded in the forms. It was only when the bishops of the Second Vatican Council (1962–65) published documents which coupled new definitions of holiness with the mandate to update and renew religious life, that the sisters felt free to shed them.

The research populations selected for this study are the two communities named above: the Dominican Sisters of Mission San

Jose, California, who trace their roots to a thirteenth-century contemplative foundation in Germany; and the Sisters of Notre Dame de Namur, who were founded in the wake of the French Revolution and who drew their inspiration from the Jesuit tradition. The Sisters of Notre Dame have a province structure; therefore samples were drawn from two governmental units, Massachusetts and California.

A total of forty sisters, twenty from each congregation, responded to a guided interview of about an hour's duration. The questions were designed to surface memories about novitiate refectories: food (quality, quantity, availability, familiarity of diet); environment (textures and colors, seating and setting); formal behaviors (reading, speaking, penances, table manners). After the sisters had thus reexplored the objects and actions in those environs, I inquired into how they had been initiated into the practices, how the unfamiliar had been explained, and what each respondent thought the purpose of all these special behaviors was. (If this differed from the mistress's explanation, I asked for clarification.) Question number 14 (see the Appendix) was the crucial one for this study: "Did these become a meaningful part of your spirituality?", a simple way of asking if the cultural orientation and the personal orientation fused. In the remaining questions I investigated diverse matters: whether the ritual had achieved its purpose (by asking where their focus of attention was during the meal), communication controls (with whom they had discussed these matters when the customs were alive), sources of change, and acceptance of change. The interviews were tape-recorded at the session and transcribed later onto data sheets. I considered emotional reactions to be part of the data and noted when anger was voiced at the memories, when respondents struggled for composure, and when they were displeased at my questions.

After congregational leaders gave me permission to do the study, they notified their members that they might be asked to take part, but participation was voluntary. I selected my subjects by their date of entrance. The Dominicans had had a General Chapter in the summer of 1961, had changed their formation director at that time, and had introduced a new post, a postulant director who was independent of, rather than an assistant to, the novice director. I made sure that some of my sample predated that change. Notre Dame's General Chapter took place in the summer of 1963, at which time both Massachusetts and California replaced their formation personnel. Another factor considered for this sample was that the

Vatican Council had already begun to issue documents aimed at updating church practice (though the document on religious life was not issued until October of 1965); in the atmosphere created by the council, Notre Dame also began to change its customs. The novices of 1963 would have entered in 1961 and 1962: I wanted to be sure I located and interviewed some of them. I arranged for some of these interviews to take place in conjunction with the Boston Province assembly in 1984 or at gatherings at the Mission San Jose mother-house in the following year, so I could include people who lived at a distance from those centers. All the interviews took place in Boston or Worcester, Massachusetts, in the Bay Area of San Francisco, or in Los Angeles, in 1984–85.

Ten subjects were drawn from those who entered each congregation between 1960 and 1964, and ten from those who entered prior to 1925. Ten people represent 43 percent of the current Dominican membership who entered between 1960 and 1964 (about 145 candidates entered in those years but only twenty-three remain). In Notre Dame ten sisters represent 12 percent of the current population drawn from those years (eighty-two women remain from the 425 candidates who entered the Massachusetts and California novitiates). Ten people represent 18 percent of the current pre-1925 Dominican population, and 13 percent of that entrance category among Sisters of Notre Dame in the two provinces being studied. I presume that the sisters who are currently members of a congregation identify more closely with its cultural orientations than those who have left. When these interviews indicate a dichotomy between personal and cultural orientations in a particular era, I assume that the gap was at least as wide among the total group as it is in the group who are now members.

Interviews were held with six formation directors in office between 1960 and 1964 (four in Notre Dame; two in the Dominicans). I inquired about the directors' qualifications for their posts, their understanding of their role, their methods of initiating new members, their observations and interpretations about the differences between their own initiation process and that of the group they supervised. The subject matter for these conversations was cumulative. Whenever a response introduced a new avenue for exploration, such as feelings of isolation, I made it a part of the conversation with the next person. I had expected to find some reluctant to answer questions about their exercise of office, but only one of the six showed any such reluctance. Most wanted to talk about that very difficult assignment at some length. Most conversations lasted about two hours; one moved closer to five hours (two sessions). Some of these formation directors were elected as delegates to General Chapters or served as provincials at other times. I asked them about the perceived need for changes and the sources of change as they saw them from those roles. In addition, I sought out a few former leaders in each community who had not been formation directors to discuss the same processes.

I am aware of the fact that I am using a vocabulary that is germane to my research population. While it might be familiar to Roman Catholics, readers who have not lived in this world might not recognize the contextual meanings, since these are drawn from monastic and scholastic realms of centuries past. I hope the ensuing glossary, one that names the persons, activities, ranks, and roles of pre–Vatican II religious life, will reduce semantic confusion.

GLOSSARY

When a candidate was first received into a congregation, she was called a "postulant." In the United States her garb was often a black, midcalf-length skirt, a long-sleeved blouse, and a cap or net veil. After a brief period (usually six months), she advanced to "novice" status and wore the distinctive clothing (called the "habit") of her order, set apart only by a white cloth veil, instead of the standard black one. In this one or two-year period she learned all the prayers and devotions practiced by her sisters and perfected her ability to engage in routine actions without losing her state of inner reflection. She was instructed in the theology of the vows she would later profess and in the history of her congregation. Study and manual labor were her occupations. Before 1965 the person responsible for training postulants and/or novices was called a "mistress." (After that time the term was often replaced by that of "formation director.") In the two congregations considered in these pages the vows that were embraced were those of "poverty, chastity, and obedience." Once those were publicly "professed," the former novice advanced to the rank of a "professed sister," although a "junior professed" was a more exact title. At this stage her vows were made for one or two years only, then renewed, giving the individual and the group leaders more leeway in regard to entering into a permanent commitment.

After eight more years, most or all of which was spent actively engaged in the congregation's official work (called "apostolate" or "mission"), the sister made permanent (or "perpetual") vows, thereby becoming a full member of the community.

All of those who entered into this process were responding to a "vocation," a perceived inner invitation to dedicate their lives totally to God. The most commonly cited biblical foundation for the existence of such vocations was the passage on the rich young man, one who kept all the commandments but who wanted to do more (Matt. 19:16–22; Mark 10:17–22). To him Jesus had said, "Go, sell all that you have, give the money to the poor and you will have treasure in heaven, then come, follow me." Only the sainted founders of religious families were trail-blazers in this regard. Once the charism was institutionalized, the members walked along a well-marked road of holy obedience.

One way in which the sisters judged the quality of their discipleship was by their adherence to the Holy Rule, the constitutions of the congregation. These treated of the essentials: the end and spirit of the Institute (which usually included the sanctification of the members and the apostolic commitment), the obligations of the vowed life, the structures of governance, disciplinary procedures. Written guidelines on matters of minor concern were collected into "customaries," "directories," or lists of "recommendations." All of the above were written or amended by sisters who were appointed or elected to be delegates to those legislative gatherings that were known as "General Chapters." These met at six-year intervals. Their decisions were promulgated as the "Acts" of the chapter.

The hierarchy consisted of "superiors" at the lowest level of organization, the local house, and moved upward to "provincials" and "mother general" in Notre Dame, the "prioress general" or simply "mother" in the Dominicans. These women were expected to model virtue and fidelity to the rules (and recommendations) and to make sure that their subordinates were likewise virtuous and faithful. Listening to self-accusation, the admission of failure in keeping the rules, was one mode of gauging the "fervor" (virtue) of the house. Such gatherings were called the "Chapter of Faults." In Notre Dame the superior or novice mistress gave an inspirational talk before the confession of fault began; therefore they named the occasion after that aspect of the meeting, calling it "conference." In addition to holding a monthly conference, Notre Dame brought self-accusation into the daily meal ritual. In the refectory naming one's fault was followed by "asking a penance." It was a whispered subject-superior exchange, visibly public, audibly private.

Notre Dame's prayer life was largely one of private meditation. It did not need a specialized vocabulary. The opposite is true of the Dominicans. Their prayer was chiefly "choral," carried out "in common" (as a community) in the chapel choir. At various hours of the day, such as at morning lauds or evening vespers, they assembled to speak, chant, sing the psalms, prayers, and hymns of the "Divine Office," the official daily prayer of the Church. The sisters faced each other across the center aisle of the chapel when engaged in this ritual, alternately standing or sitting, sometimes bowing slightly or profoundly on designated phrases. The person charged with beginning the prayer at each hour that week was called the "hebdomadarian." The "versicularian" was a soloist who intoned a verse from the psalms to which the community then responded. It was their prayer in chapel that the Dominicans brought to their meals. Their confession of fault was embodied gesturally, carried out in silence. Called the "venia," it was a stylized movement that involved "prostrating" (lying down on the floor), turning on one's side and covering one's face with one's "scapular" (sleeveless outer garment that hung from the shoulders).

These terms are the stepping stones into the fifteen-hundred-year-old ascetic tradition to which the Dominicans and the Sisters of Notre Dame belonged.

This research draws heavily on the actors' interpretations of their reality, but the interpretation of the whole reaches into a wide range of material from history, theology, and symbolic anthropology: ascetic food beliefs and the question of boundary; the tension between body/spirit, time/eternity in Catholic theology and in Jesuit and Dominican spiritualities; the celibate state and gender categories; the relationship between environmental design and social structure; the secularization of the discourse on body; the movement from self-discipline to self-expression as an American cultural ideal; the movement from withdrawal to engagement as a Roman Catholic ideal; the absence of ritual and its effects on convent culture.

The key to the convent refectory opens the door to a common heritage, for the grace before meals is a chant about the body and soul in Western culture.

PART ONE

THE COMMON MEAL

1

FOOD RITUAL:
DOMINICAN SISTERS OF
MISSION SAN JOSE

The Dominican Sisters of Mission San Jose, formally known as the Congregation of the Queen of the Holy Rosary, date their beginnings to 1876, the year Mother Pia Backes and two companions were sent from Brooklyn to San Francisco to teach the children of the German-speaking Catholics in that city. At that time Mother Pia belonged to the Amityville Dominicans, who in turn traced their roots to the revered Convent of the Holy Cross in Ratisbon (now Regensburg), Germany. Ratisbon was founded in 1233, shortly after the death of St. Dominic, and its fame stems from its thirteenth-century origins, its uninterrupted history, and the fact that twelve Dominican congregations in the United States trace their roots to this one source (Mehegan 1976: 2–10).

In California it became apparent that decision making by Brooklyn was an ineffective model of governance, especially as an exchange of letters took weeks. In 1888, therefore, the western group separated and within two years won affiliation with the Dominican Order as the Congregation of the Queen of the Holy Rosary. Before Mother Pia's death in 1925 the community had opened eighteen elementary and four secondary schools in California and Oregon and had made several foundations in Mexico. Vocations were recruited not only from these sources but from Germany as well. Many young women became missionaries to the United States after their formation in Moresnet-Neutre (in present-day Belgium) or at Altenhohenau in Bavaria, where the novitiate moved in 1923.

In 1963, the focal point of this study, there were 575 professed members in this congregation. Most of these worked in the five

3

child-care institutions, thirty-three grade schools or nine high schools they staffed (*Official Catholic Directory* 1963: 905; Brown 1967: 4, 988).

Mission San Jose, 1963

The motherhouse complex of the Dominican Sisters is set on a hillside overlooking an eighteenth-century Franciscan mission, Mission San Jose, in California. In 1963, its buildings housed approximately 130 sisters in formation, professed, and retirement communities, as well as five or six workmen in cottages. A college for the newly professed (juniorate), a Catholic grammar school, and the administrative staff of the congregation operated on the premises. Aspirants entered the motherhouse and most of them spent four years on these grounds as postulants, novices, and junior professed before being sent to another house on mission.

My purpose in the next few pages is to reconstruct for the reader the shape of the Dominican's dining ritual. My description derives from interviews with members and from community documents, revised until judged accurate by the members. For the sake of clarity in presentation I have adopted the voice of an omniscient viewer. The scene is a midday dinner in Lent of 1963.

Noon vespers have ended. As sisters leave their places in choir to form their processional lines, those who need to move ahead to prepare for public penance or to assume refectory chores kiss the scapular of their habit as they pass the prioress. In so doing they have asked to be excused from the continuing community prayer.

Entering the atrium, the novices and professed hang up their long black woolen mantles and reassemble by rank in prayerful silence. The postulants who lead the procession are clothed totally in black: midcalf-length, pleated cotton skirts, blouse, short cape, nylons, and laced shoes. The novices wear the familiar Dominican white habit, full-length rosary looped through a black belt; a white veil their novice sign. The professed follow the novices, those of highest rank occupying the last places—the general councillors, the past and the present prioress general. The latter intones the familiar Psalm 129, "De profundis clamavi ad te Domini," and the sisters continue the antiphonal Latin prayer, thus interceding for the deceased in purgatory.

The lines move on. Outside the refectory door the penitents kneel. On this particular day some hold up fragments of an object they have broken, one holds her finger over compressed lips, yet another raises her arms in prayer. The first pair of postulants stops at the doorway facing the kneeling figures. Mother walks down the center of the lengthy procession, enters the refectory, and gently pulls the slender bell rope signaling the community to enter.

Again the line moves on. Each pair walks side by side past the penitents, over the threshold, down the middle of the room. Together they make a head inclination to the crucifix hanging above the prioress's place on the farthest wall of the bare, rectangular room; then reversing direction, they again walk the length of the refectory to form lines of religious rank with the youngest at the foot of the room.

Standing in the doorway at the foot of the refectory one can see windows dressed in white half curtains which look out on a covered walkway. There are similar windows on the opposite end, the wall of the interior corridor. No bright colors catch the eye. The original wooden floor is covered in brown linoleum: the walls are painted white. Sturdy but simple wooden tables and benches, hewn in the motherhouse carpentry shop, line the walls. Halfway down on the left side the tables are separated by a handsome pulpit carved by the skilled hands of a German sister. The head table is raised on a dais: seated here will be the prioress general, the ex–prioress general, and three of the general councillors. Parallel to this head table and in front of it is the vortisch (penance table), whose bench is barely a foot high. This wooden table, like the others, is covered with a cream-colored linoleum, but unlike the others stands but two feet high. Those not yet perfected in custody of the eyes have glanced at the napkin ring as they passed by in procession to read the name of the one who will take her meal here.

In a Dominican refectory tables should line three walls, but here in Mission San Jose vocations have been so high in the past few years that two extra tables are set in the center of the lower end of the room, and contrary to tradition, postulants and novices will sit on both sides facing each other.

The versicularian for the week intones "Benedicite" and the Latin prayers begin. (I have used the English translation from *Dominican Community Prayers*, 1966, and noted accompanying body postures in brackets in the following text.)

Chantress: The poor will eat and receive their fill.

Community: Those who seek the Lord will praise him and will live forever. Glory be to the Father, to the Son and the Holy Spirit. [During this last line the sisters incline forward and place their hands on their knees. They rise on the next line.] As it was in the beginning, is now, and ever shall be. Lord, have mercy. Christ, have mercy. Lord, have mercy. [Now the sisters make a profound inclination; while bowing they place their crossed arms on their knees as they silently recite an "Our Father." They rise.]

Hebdomadarian: And lead us not into temptation.

Comm.: But deliver us from evil.

Heb.: Let us pray. Bless, O Lord, these Thy gifts which we are about to receive from Thy bounty. Through Christ Our Lord.

Comm.: Amen.

Reader: Pray, a blessing.

Heb.: May the King of everlasting glory bring us to His heavenly banquet.

Comm.: Amen.

With an economy of movement and a perfected silence of action each one assumes her place, sits upright, hands folded beneath the scapular, head bowed. The stillness is broken by the reader's voice: "Dear Mothers and Sisters, seat with you at table the soul which has the most to suffer and regale it with an Our Father and a Hail Mary." Then she kneels on the top step of the pulpit. Servers kneel at the doorway while praying for the holy souls in purgatory. Assuming an upright stance the reader announces the chapter and verse of that day's gospel passage and is seated at the microphone to read it.

Then the refectory stage comes alive. Simultaneously Dominican sisters play out their prescribed parts in solo, duet, or company roles.

Two novices, called "angels" in this role, process down the center carrying baskets full of bread. The bread is divided into packets of four or five slices, wrapped in waxed paper. Together the sisters incline to the crucifix and distribute their ritual gifts, placing a packet between every other setting, beginning with the youngest at the lower end of the table.

As they do so, the seated unroll their white cloth napkins containing their silverware and gently place their service on the table top, careful lest a sound distract from the reading. Then they lift their white dinner plates and place napkins underneath as placemats, letting much of the fullness fall over the edge to cover their laps. The other end is tucked under the chin. As the dessert (usually fruit) and salad servings are already at their places, the company awaits the individual servings of soup, vegetable, and main dish. On this Lenten Monday the menu consists of wine soup, veal sausage, boiled potato, baked squash, apricots, and tea.

The reader has finished the gospel passage and continues on to the prescribed Monday selection, "The Rule of St. Augustine," upon which Dominican constitutions are based. The professed know it by heart. A slip of the tongue, an omission of a phrase, would indeed be public faults and the sister appointed to monitor the reading would record the errors and give the list of corrections to the reader at the end of the meal.

The servers, who wear long white aprons and half sleeves to protect the habit, go about their tasks efficiently. The quickness of their pace is tempered only by their experience, having seen hasty hands lose their grip on the heavy trays.

When most of the sisters have been served, the prioress general knocks on the wooden table; that sound is the signal to eat. Once the main course is finished those who wish to be served tea turn their cups upright. They then draw their cups and saucers toward them if they do not want another sister to add hot milk to their tea. Twenty minutes have elapsed from the sound of the knock. The prioress general again surveys the scene and rings the bell to signal the end of dining. At that bell the reader rises and sings: "Tu autem, Domine, miserere nostri." The community responds, "Deo gratias."

There is a task for everyone to perform now. The untouched food must be collected to be reused later; the scraps disposed. Some sisters collect the bread, others the individual servings of vegetable or meat that a few older professed did not eat, or from which they put but a small portion on their plates. In the kitchen a multilayered cart containing dishpans filled with steaming hot water is wheeled to the slide so the pans can be passed through the window. These are placed on the tables at intervals of four sisters who divide the tasks of washing, rinsing, and drying. Only the sister at the penance table has hers done for her. The dishpans are removed, the silverware rolled in the napkins, the penance table carried out. At the knock they once more form two rows facing each other across the center space to sing the grace after meals. When the lines are formed there is a sensed moment of readiness and all those who were formal penitents make the venia: they prostrate, turn to the side, and draw the scapular over the face. Those who committed a fault during the meal (spilling the tea, dropping the silverware) kiss the floor. These rise and join the lines and the grace begins. As in the previous grace they make a middle inclination at the doxology and a profound inclination during the "Our Father.")

Chantress: The kind and compassionate Lord has left us a memorial of his wondrous deeds.

All: He has given food to all who live in holy fear.

Hebdomadarian: We give you thanks, almighty God, for all your gifts, who live and reign forever.

[The community chants antiphonally the following "Miserere."]

—Have mercy on me, O God, in your goodness;

—In the greatness of your compassion wipe out my offense.

—Thoroughly wash me from my guilt and of my sin cleanse me.

—For I acknowledge my offense, and my sin is before me always:

—Against you only have I sinned, and done what is evil in your sight.

—That you may be justified in your sentence, vindicated when you condemn.

—Indeed, in guilt was I born, and in sin my mother conceived me;

—Behold, you are pleased with sincerity of heart, and in my inmost being you teach me wisdom.

—Cleanse me of sin with hyssop, that I may be purified; wash me and I shall be whiter than snow.

—Let me hear the sounds of joy and gladness; the bones you have crushed shall rejoice.

—Turn away your face from my sins, and blot out all my guilt.

—A clean heart create for me, O God, and a steadfast spirit renew within me. Cast me not out from your presence, and your holy spirit take not from me.

—Give me back the joy of your salvation, and a willing spirit sustain in me.

—I will teach transgressors your ways, and sinners shall return to you.

—Free me from blood guilt, O God, my saving God; then my tongue shall revel in your justice.

—O Lord, open my lips, and my mouth shall proclaim your praise.

—For you are not pleased with sacrifices; should I offer a holocaust you would not accept it.

—My sacrifice, O God, is a contrite spirit; a heart contrite and humbled, O God, you will not spurn.

—Be bountiful, O Lord, to Sion in your kindness by rebuilding the walls of Jerusalem;

—Then shall you be pleased with due sacrifices, burnt offerings and holocausts; then shall they offer up bullocks on your altar.

—Glory be to the Father and to the Son, and to the Holy Spirit,

—As it was in the beginning, is now and ever shall be, world without end. Amen.

[A silent "Our Father" is prayed here.]

Heb.: He has been generous to the poor.

All:　His goodness is everlasting.

Heb.: I will bless the Lord at all times.

All:　His praises are ever on my lips.

Heb.: My soul will exult in the Lord.

All:　The meek will hear it with gladness.

Heb.: Praise the Lord with me.

All:　Together let us extol his name.

Heb.: Blessed be the name of the Lord.

All:　Both now and forevermore.

Heb.: O Lord, reward with everlasting life all those who do good to us in your name.

All:　Amen.

Heb.: Let us bless the Lord.

All:　Thanks be to God.

The movement patterns accompanying the above vocal arrangements are equally powerful yet utterly simple. The first penance occurs during the "Miserere" prayer. Four professed, two on either side, begin to kiss the feet of their sisters. They kneel to kiss the tip of the shoe and when they feel the touch of the hands on their shoulders they rise, step backward, and repeat. The more lithesome carry a rhythm in the rising and the falling that melds into that of the chant.

Others select a variety of body gestures as they kneel: one drops a few inches of her black woolen veil over her eyes; a few others take positions used by the penitents at the doorway on this Lenten Monday. When the hebdomadarian begins the prayer, "O Lord, reward with everlasting life . . . " all of these make the venia. During the response to this prayer a knock is given for them to rise.

The two lines now meet in the center of the room and move forward to the center crucifix; the oldest sisters turn right and left and lead the double line out of the room. In the corridor they divide; some go to work in the kitchen, others remain in line until they reach their respective recreation rooms—separate areas for postulants, novices, and professed.

Ritual Guidelines: Constitutions and Customaries

Every Dominican constitution is based on the Rule of St. Augustine. It precedes every edition of the constitutions of this congregation. Whereas a few articles from the constitutions were read each day so that the whole was covered twice annually, it was the Rule that was read in its entirety each Monday. Consequently the sisters knew it by heart. So it is to this document that I first turn for foundational attitudes toward the meal.

St. Augustine looked to the Acts of the Apostles for his norm for food distribution. In the light of this text he counseled superiors to give to each one according to her needs (as opposed to giving equally to all). It is clear from the spiritual advice that followed that he realized the potential hazards of living out this norm in community. He simultaneously discouraged all forms of comparative living and encouraged a value system that prized fast and abstinence over satisfaction. Mortification of the appetite, however, was never to be pursued to the detriment of good health.

When speaking specifically of the common meal St. Augustine

required that all "listen without noise and contention to that which is read to you according to custom, until you rise from your meal; nor let your mouth only receive food, but let your ears also be fed with the Word of God" (OP 1952: 27).

Both customaries and constitutions attend to this original agenda: respecting refectory silence, listening to the Word, being present at the common meal, fast and abstinence. A second set of agenda items was inherited from the order.

The first customary of this congregation ("Ceremonial of the Congregation of the Queen of the Most Holy Rosary of the Third Order of St. Dominic, est. 1910"), a handwritten, handsewn booklet, explicates the connections between the regulations around food and the Dominican sources for those regulations.

Chapter 4, "Of the Refectory and the Meals," opens with the statement tht the refectory is subject to "several prescriptions emanating from the Chapters General of the [First] Order" (OP 1910: 10). The primary command is that the refectory is a place of silence. If communication becomes necessary it should be done in sign. If signs are insufficient, a few words may be pronounced in a low tone. Reference is made to a Chapter General held in Rome in 1650 where superiors were prohibited from correcting their subjects in their respective refectories; such corrections were deemed an abuse of silence. In order to protect and promote the desired atmosphere only silent penances could be performed, e.g., venia, and these only for two reasons—for grave faults or on the eve of a great feast. And even these, the directive cautioned, "should not be multiplied lest confusion arise thereby during the repast and the refectory be deprived of its principal end" (11).

The second topic treated in this document is the order of seating and the placement of furniture. It is specified that the tables be arranged near the walls so as to form a horseshoe and the sisters occupy but one side of the tables, facing the center of the room. Dominican convents for men and women followed this pattern. The places reserved for the prioress and the subprioress were to correspond to their places at the Choir of the Office and the Chapter. Sisters dispensed from the abstinence (allowed to eat meat) were to sit at a separate table—the only exception possible would be that of the prioress, who even if dispensed, must preside over the meal.

Many of the ritual behaviors described earlier in this study are mandated here. Compulsory behaviors referred to in the customary include assembling in the atrium or vestibule and processing into the refectory; partaking in prayers before meals; listening to verses from Holy Scripture; following a ritualized distribution of bread. The brief explanation of the latter practice offered here is as follows:

In commemoration of the miraculous loaves which the angels brought to our Blessed Father St. Dominic, and his companions in the refectory of St. Sixtus in Rome, two young sisters, at the beginning of the midday and evening meal, (not at the collation) bring each a basket of bread, which they distribute, one on the right side, the other on the left, beginning at the lower end, and advancing towards the Prioress and the Subprioress, whom after having finished the distribution they together salute, by an inclination of the head. (OP 1910: 13)

The agenda inherited from the Dominican Friars Preachers concerned this myth and its ritual, ceremonial forms, and an environment ordered by rank.

In regard to the food itself, the customary instructs the prioress to procure food of good quality and sufficient quantity. Sufficient quantity is translated into soup and two to three dishes for dinner; two dishes for supper. On days of celebration one more course is permitted either as a main dish or as dessert. The morning collation on fast days was limited to two ounces of food, exclusive of liquid. Except for those dispensed the food had to be the same for all.

Other concerns were that the refectory should be locked when not in use; that even when open, no one should enter without permission; that it should be "resplendent with cleanliness" (12). The tables were to be set in such a way that whatever the sisters needed during the meal, that is, water, bread, and salt, were to be within reach.

One action prescribed by this document (changed by the Chapter of 1961) was a ritual washing of the hands that took place as the sisters processed from the atrium to the refectory. Every convent built before 1961 has a sink in a corridor adjacent to the dining room, a silent architectural testimony to the existence of this centuries-old custom.

A major area of concern was the reading. Both content and execution were important. The prioress was held responsible for consulting competent people in selecting books that were both doctrinally sound and edifying. Whereas old works on the history and saints of the order were to be respected, out-of-date or poorly written books were not, lest they "give a wrong bias to the literary taste of the nuns" (OP 1910: 14). The reader was permitted to prepare the selection in advance and to consult a dictionary kept at the podium to find the correct pronunciation, but if an error was made a sister would correct her. This practice took precedence over the general rule mentioned above that superiors were not to correct subjects in the refectory. If the reader's pace was too quick, the prioress was to rap the table as a signal for her to slow down.

The concluding section addressed the individual—the self-discipline she was expected to observe and the religious motivation appropriate to the discipline. She was exhorted to maintain a "proper, edifying and truly religious exterior" by avoiding any hastiness in taking food, any abruptness in movements, any indication of likes or dislikes whether of reading matter or of food, any singularity, any curiosity regarding her neighbor (though she should be attentive to the needs of that neighbor) (14).

Up until this point historical justification of the customs was drawn from the seventeenth and eighteenth-century Chapters of the Friars Preachers. But here the spirituality turned to the "Following of Christ." A passage from that collection of spiritual sayings was quoted that warned against becoming a slave to the needs of the body because those needs are a burden to the fervent soul. Lest the sisters err on the other extreme by ignoring the needs of the body and becoming ill thereby, they are reminded that the health of the body is beneficial to that of the soul; therefore, the customary concludes, no one may decide to practice private mortification without the permission of her superior. In fact, everyone had to take a portion from each dish unless a particular dish made her ill. From all of the above it is clear that while asceticism was prized, it could not be pursued to the detriment of the body or at the whim of the individual.

The tension between asceticism and indulgence was a common concern for all Catholic traditions, so spiritual writers borrowed from varied sources for inspiration and insight. Hyacinth Cormier, OP, an ex–master general and a friend of Mother Pia, wrote a spiritual guide published at Mission San Jose which illustrates the aforementioned pooling of religious knowledge. He looks outside the Dominican tradition for the principles of moderation in eating and drinking. St. Francis de Sales provides the first principle: "We must eat to live, not live to eat." St. Gregory provides the second:

"Without the mortification of the palate, there is no thought of spiritual progress" (Cormier et al. 1916: 95). Mortification was a condition for spiritual progress but moderation was the means. According to Cormier moderation facilitated a state of being that was marked by simplicity, freedom, and gratitude toward God. Most important, it "affords the opportunity of thinking during meals on the greater honor and glory of God. In this way, we shall begin to taste the sweetness of Heaven, which consists not in eating and drinking but rather in the peace and joy of the Holy Ghost" (96). In summary, eating was a highly charged activity. Indulgence of the body weighed down the soul; mortification of the body freed the mind and spirit for contemplation of the holy—a foretaste of eternity.

This customary expanded on some of the congregational regulations enumerated in the Constitutions of 1908, articles 181–96. Some basic policies set down only in the latter document are that since the sisters need their strength for teaching, they will not follow customs of fasting peculiar to the order, but only those of the Church, with some congregational exceptions. The congregation practiced abstinence from meat on Wednesdays, Fridays, and Saturdays. In addition to abstinence, fasting between meals was to be observed on Fridays (the strong could fast on bread and water on Good Friday) and on the eve of the feast of St. Dominic.

Other regulations made it clear that there were to be only two sittings per meal (called first and second table). All meals were to be taken in the refectory and the prioress could not dispense sisters from being at first table without good reason; nor could she ever dispense from silence there. As for the food, it was to be nourishing, well prepared, and sufficiently abundant without being "choice" (article 186,81). A sister could pass an unused portion to the person on her right or left but could not send it anywhere else.

Only one aspect of the table setting is mentioned (not under refectory rules but under those of poverty): that the use of silver spoons was allowed (article 162, 75). Noteworthy here is the huge painting of St. Dominic giving wooden spoons to the first group of Dominican sisters that hangs on the walls of the motherhouse corridor just outside the archives. His care and concern for the sisters was retained as significant; the fact that the spoons were wooden was not. Evidently the use of silver articles multiplied after the 1908 permission, and in the next edition of the constitutions permission to use silver utensils was withdrawn (1923: article 133,103).

The Constitutions of 1908 are the only ones to speak of table manners. They are mentioned as part of the behavioral training for which the novice mistress was responsible. She was to make sure that the sisters ate "decorously, without avidity and properly, so as not to disgust those around them" (article 93,59).

In the 1923, 1937, and 1952 editions these refectory regulations were restated, rephrased, or reemphasized, but little was changed. The reasons for rank and order were elaborated in a document commenting on the 1923 Constitutions.

The correct order of precedence is a matter of great importance in a religious community. In Heaven the celestial choirs are grouped according to rank and order. The Saints too occupy the places assigned to them. The visible Church upon earth regulates minutely the order of her hierarchy, from the humble acolyte to the Vicar of Christ. The same is true in human society, even within the narrow limits of the family circle. Disregard or neglect of this custom would everywhere result in chaotic confusion. (OP archives, c. 1923)

Clearly this is not an attempt to offer a contemporary rationale, but to reassert the traditional outlook of the order of Friars Preachers. Safeguarding this tradition was stressed. In the introduction to the 1943 *Acts of the General Chapter* an anonymous Dominican Father is quoted as saying that change should not be lightly introduced and that whereas it is true that constitutions can be changed, such changes should be in the spirit of those constitutions; otherwise a congregation might be no longer Dominican (OP 1943: 7).

Maintaining a genuine Dominican identity was an ongoing concern. The 1937 Customary states that Mother Frances Raphael Drane's *Spirit of the Dominican Order* would be read annually, as would a life of St. Dominic. In addition, the account of the death of St. Dominic should be read on the eve of his feast (OP 1937: 83). An unwritten practice of the congregation (derived from that of the First Order) was to read an account of the last illness and death of each of their members as soon as one could be drawn up. These spoke of how the deceased had met death, her resignation to God's will, and how the community prayers and rites of the church had assisted her at that time. Later another account was written that included her early family history, her decision to enter religious life, favored hymns or prayers, her fidelity to community prayers, some personal characteristic, the manner of her death. If the moment of death occurred while tower bells chimed or while the sisters were singing a "Salve Regina," for example, this synchronism was recorded. These life histories were gathered together in one volume every six years and the whole was read annually for the next six years (the space of time between General Chapters). For example, the "Necrology of 1961–1967" contains the lives of thirty-nine sisters. This volume would be read in the refectory each year until 1973. Sisters were also indexed by date of death so the reader could remember each one on the eve of her anniversary. At those times only the one sentence was proclaimed. I take an illustration from 1963, "Sister M. Petrina Tannenheimer of the Holy Spirit died January 2, 1963, in the 81st year of her age and the 54th year of her religious profession" (OP 1967). Such practices bridged this world and the next, reminding the living that evolutionary time was but a prologue to eschatological time and that the life of virtue was unending.

No major changes were made in the first half of the twentieth century in refectory customs, but some items rather peripheral to the rules and constitutions were introduced. The clearest example of this is the use of the tablecloth. In 1937 this was tied to the singing of the "Laudate." Tablecloths were thereby required for dinner on all Sundays except those of Advent and Lent (forty-two Sundays) and for twenty-two other feast days. But in 1955 the sisters' chapter lowered this number from sixty-four occasions to five, specifying that the cloth be used for all three meals (OP 1955: 10). In the 1937 Customary a breakfast menu and its variations were given. On ordinary days the breakfast was to consist of fruit, cereal, bread and butter, coffee and milk. On feast days and Sundays cake, meat, or eggs could be added. This particular customary was so orderly and detailed that my opening description of a meal could almost have been based on this one document.

Missing from all of these constitutions, commentaries, and chapter acts are descriptions of and regulations for refectory penances. Membership interviews are the only source for garnering this information. These interviews reveal that few penances were practiced outside of Advent and Lent, the heaviest use being in Lent.

One penance that was performed all year long was kneeling at the doorway with whatever object one had broken or treated improperly (e.g., holding a sweater if one had left it overnight in the community room). The sister would have first seen the superior of the house to confess her fault verbally before taking her place at the door to confess it visually to the community.

Another yearlong practice was to make the venia at the end of the meal for a fault committed during the meal (e.g., dropping a bowl of food).

The vortisch (or little table) could be used at any point in the year, but if it was used outside of a penitential season it had only one interpretation—the person sitting at it had been assigned there because of some rather serious fault and her superior had decided that the subject's correction should also be public. The sister at fault would have to go to the refectorian before the meal to ask her to set that table and place it in the center of the room. In Lent, however, there was another possible interpretation—that the individual wished to practice a difficult penance for her own spiritual development.

Some penances fell out of use naturally, that is, no one chose to enact them and they were not assigned by the prioress from the Chapter of Faults. One of these was begging soup. This involved kneeling on the unoccupied side of the table across from the seated community, extending a soup bowl for contributions from the individual portions of the sisters, moving to the center of the room, and kneeling beneath the crucifix to consume the contents of the bowl. One person remembered seeing it in the early 1960s at the mother-house, but many others said that in fact it had gone out of practice long before in the local houses.

One penance that seems to have stopped in the 1950s was lying on the threshold of the refectory while sisters stepped over the penitent. Again, the individual would have chosen to do this.

In the novitiate the newer members were encouraged to try each of the penances in use. This encouragement was the only congregational guideline on frequency.

Transmitting the Meal Tradition

Two new formation directors took office in 1961. One would remain in that position for fifteen years, the other would serve for six years but return to formation work at a later time.[1] As was common in the practice of religious life in this era, both were appointed to their tasks without prior consultation and without receiving any special preparation. They met with the outgoing mistress for two hours and attended a three-day workshop in Albany, New York, with Father

Elio Gambari from the Sacred Congregation of Religious in Rome. Among other things, he told the group that Rome wanted religious women to modernize and update their customs.

The directors' appointed task, however, was not to initiate agenda for General Chapters on changing religious life, but to train newer members to the life as it existed.

On the first day of their terms they conferred with each other on whether to teach what they were taught or to do what they thought best. One of them recounted some experiences she had had in her novitiate that she had found distressing and they agreed not to act in that manner. Aside from agreeing not to repeat certain styles of behavior, they decided to use their judgment as they went along about how to pass on what they had been taught. After that conversation and the shared workshop, they worked independently for the duration of their common term of office—one with the novices and the other with the postulants.

They did not know that they had different viewpoints on penance—differences that affected both their explanations and their interactions with newer members who questioned the customs.

One mistress had always found the customary penances personally repulsive, but she conformed in order to be a member of the group, and she was willing to accept the idea that they led to holiness. She remembered thinking that they humbled those who practiced them—and humility was a virtue. Besides, they went against nature, were painful, and were therefore helpful. Whatever went against nature or was painful could be offered up to God in union with the sacrifice of Jesus on the cross.

In each entrance group she found three or four novices who said they could not or would not take part. As a matter of policy she never mentioned her own difficulties, lest her attitudes inhibit another from accepting a practice as part of her monastic background. She reconstructed a typical response she might have given to one who questioned the disciplinary practices: "Just because something goes against the grain doesn't mean it isn't good for you or it isn't a good thing to do. So why don't you offer it up for some good purpose? Maybe the fact that you are doing something you don't like would help another person get a certain grace." That seemed to persuade the questioner to make a new effort. In the end they had to make the effort if they wished to remain in religious life.

The other mistress always considered penances to be healthy;

sometimes she misses them now. They had a way, she said, of making one aware of innate pride. The value she saw in them was the same value her mistress had seen and taught: they exposed pride and aided the development of humility. On being asked to reconstruct a possible response to someone who was having difficulty with the practices, she suggested the following: "Pride is subtle. It creeps into so many actions. The very fact that these disciplinary practices cause complaint is proof that one's pride is very sensitive. Unite your pain or discomfort to Our Lord who suffered so much on our behalf and who in His Passion was so openly ridiculed. In the spirit of Lent, conform yourself to that image." When such an explanation was given, she recalled, the resistant seemed more accepting.

Before Advent began, the postulants were told they would be seeing the novices and the professed taking part in disciplinary practices proper to seasons of penance. Then the mistress would both demonstrate and explain what was involved. The novitiate would also include instructions on these customs.

Half the Dominican candidates interviewed who entered between 1960 and 1964 (five) named penance and/or humility as the key concept behind the practices. Most who named penance were confused by the question that followed: "For whom?" After a period of hesitation one said she thought it was for past sinfulness; another for the sins of the world; another for the condition of sinfulness in general. Other memories of explanations that surfaced included the idea of being in continuity with the tradition of the order; being in union with Christ; self-offering. Just one sister had no memory of any explanation, although she was sure there was one. The whole thing was so strange, she said, she was never able to remember what it was supposed to mean.

Half of those interviewed (five) said they integrated some or all of the practices into their spirituality. Of these one was enthusiastic. In her case all these rituals and disciplinary practices enabled her to externalize her spirituality and bear witness to her beliefs. She found song, communal recitation of prayer, the rhythms of standing, kneeling, bowing, and kissing the feet of the sisters fulfilling.

One named selected practices as meaningful for her, while another said individually none had meaning, but being in continuity with the monastic past gave all of them value.

A fourth sister said that at first she viewed them as old-fashioned, like the washbasins and pitchers. But she tried to give herself fully to the experience of this aspect of monastic/ascetic culture and in so doing decided they made her 'pleasing to God'; a notion she later rejected.

The last claimed they helped her get into the spirit of the liturgical season and perhaps helped her gain humility.

In the other half of the group, four said that penances never became a part of them; one was unsure. Those who rejected them saw them as unnatural, imposed, in conflict with the general United States culture which valued the person as she was. Three of these entered in 1964: one told me they earned the dubious reputation of being the first class to question the value of self-discipline in itself.

Most of the elder sisters expected and looked forward to a distinctively different lifestyle marked by discipline and some austerity.[2]

In respect to the special practices of dining, these ten sisters had learned about penances and had been initiated into them in a variety of ways. One had been a boarder in a school belonging to this congregation. Other students there had peered into the refectory secretly and reported the practices (with some embellishments) to their peers. Another sister said that her entrance group ate in the parlor the first night and enough explanation was given that they were able to join the community at meals the next day. Yet another said that as postulants they ate at the second table where no penances were performed, but she arrived early one day and saw a novice kneeling in the middle of the floor. Others learned about them at instruction from the mistress during the course of the postulate. Only one of the ten reported that she was initially frightened.

Two sisters no longer remembered the timing of initiation and it is interesting that neither of them remembered if any explanation was ever given. They made it clear that they entered for the difference; explanations were not necessary. Novices did not expect or want explanations, one of them said, because people entered to learn obedience: poverty and chastity were already part of one's heritage from home. Doing things without explanation was a necessary step toward living without being governed by one's own opinions. The other sister maintained that the customs were disciplinary measures, indispensable conditions for the acquisition of contemplation. Whether they disciplined the will or the senses, she treasured them as means toward achieving that end.

The remaining eight sisters who entered in the first quarter of the century cited a variety of interpretations. The greater number focused on penance and reparation as an ingredient of monastic tradition, while a few mentioned humility also. The major penance for all, however, was not a voluntary practice of the penitential season, but the perpetual silence of the refectory. It was to this that they constantly referred when speaking of the penitential aspects of religious life.

Clearly these elder sisters chose penance when they chose religious life. Some selected this congregation, known informally as the German Dominicans, because it had the reputation of being the strictest available congregation. All ten held that the spirituality exemplified in the practices of dining was meaningful to them and had been integrated into their lives: eight were emphatic on this point. Reasons given showed considerable variety: silence was a means to interior recollection; acts of penance helped to atone for one's faults and for the sins of the souls in purgatory; it was good to do hard things; discipline is a quality of a good life.

One individual's responses did not fit into the overall pattern and need a separate telling. She was the only one in her cohort category (entered 1914–25) to distinguish in interview between what she was told and what she thought. In regard to voluntary penances, she was instructed to unite her sufferings to those of Christ, which she did. However, the real purpose of the practices, as she saw it, was to mold the members into a ready obedience so that in every circumstance they would fit into the scheme of what needed to be done. Penances and acts of mortification, therefore, exercised the members into the spirit of the vow of obedience. In her view the active life in local communities replaced the need for voluntary penances. The practices were meaningful to her insofar as they had prepared her to bear the penance of life.

On the question of whether the special behaviors of the refectory became a meaningful part of the sisters' lives, the comparative results can be tabulated in the following manner.

	Pre-1925	Post-1960
Definite yes	8	1
Qualified yes	2	4
Qualified no	0	1
Definite no	0	3
Unsure	0	1

Another aspect of the comparative data emerged from the informal interview. Each respondent knew I had the permission of the congregation to conduct a study on the rituals of convent dining. In addition, I opened each session with some statement on my present situation: that I was a Ph.D. student at the Graduate Theological Union interested in the anthropology of religion and that this interview was data for my dissertation. Yet when I asked my first question ("Did you like the food when you first entered?"), some elder sisters were startled and confused. They had never had that question asked of them and could not understand how another vowed religious could entertain it. Some seemed to perceive it as inappropriate—as if they had chosen religious life for its good food. One corrected me for my irreligious attitude. Through such interactions and resultant conversations, it became clear to me that even as postulants these elder sisters were motivated by a desire to live austerely and to do what was difficult. These were the marks of Christian love and the sign of a vocation.

Those who entered before 1925 valued what was difficult. Those who entered between 1960 and 1964 valued what was natural. For the older set the disciplined life set them free. Many of the younger ones, however, said that they maintained their freedom by conforming externally but by retaining a definition of self that differed from the one the customs taught. They saw the practices as a part of monastic life but not as a means to a higher end. In fact, the four in the younger set who said that the practices never became a meaningful part of their spirituality doubted the ability of formal behaviors to mold anyone's internal dispositions.

The tabulated responses show that in the course of the twentieth century a significant erosion occurred in the ability of the members to own the refectory customs as a meaningful part of their lives. Interview data suggest that even when the same category of response was chosen by the younger members, they chose it for reasons peculiar to their age group, or they had different attitudes toward this aspect of their past. Two who gave a "qualified yes" to the question on whether the special behaviors became a meaningful part of their spirituality were often convulsed in laughter when remembering various incidents that resulted in one of their friends being assigned a penance. Their manner of reacting to the question set them apart from their elders who chose that same category of response: none of them had connected humor with the penitential life. Another sister in the younger set valued the customs as door-ways to the sacred, as a mode of entering into the spirit of the liturgical season. None of the elder sisters articulated such a position.

2

FOOD RITUAL:
SISTERS OF NOTRE DAME
DE NAMUR

The congregation known as the Sisters of Notre Dame de Namur began in France in 1804 when a group of women led by Julie Billiart dedicated themselves to the instruction of poor children. Like other successful founders of the period, Julie Billiart was a strong, complex personality "who combined great spiritual abilities with a developed sense of action and organization" (Jedin and Dolan 1980: 206). Her congregation permitted no class distinctions among the sisters (i.e., choir and lay) and was centrally organized under one superior general. To preserve her autonomy and this mode of governance she left France to establish her motherhouse in Namur, Belgium.

In 1840 the Belgian motherhouse sent missionaries to Cincinnati, Ohio. This foundation grew rapidly and expanded eastward, resulting in the separate provinces of Massachusetts (now Ipswich and Boston), Maryland, and Connecticut. In 1846 eight more missionaries sailed from Belgium to Oregon with Pierre De Smet, SJ, to work with the Native Americans. The gold rush brought a massive population influx to California, however, so the sisters moved their headquarters to that state in 1851.

In 1963, the focal point of this investigation, there were approximately five thousand professed Sisters of Notre Dame de Namur located in Belgium, France, the British Isles, Africa, Japan, and North and South America. Almost three thousand of these were in the United States. The Massachusetts province alone had more than a thousand professed members, most of whom worked in their educational institutions, which included one college, twenty high schools and forty-two grammar schools. The California province numbered 410 sisters who staffed one college, eight high schools and thirty-two grammar schools (*Official Catholic Directory:* 921; Bland 1967: 529–30).

Ipswich, 1963

In 1962 the Massachusetts province of the Sisters of Notre Dame de Namur moved its formation program and provincial house from its cramped and crumbling quarters in the city of Waltham to a newly erected mammoth brick building in the seacoast town of Ipswich. The sisters' new home dominated the hillside just a minute's drive from the white Congregational church and common green that mark the heart of a colonial New England town; the brick and the wood a visual contrast of alien traditions, a visual statement on the shift of power. The center of the three-story brick structure held the facilities for common use: a chapel of marbled beauty and stained-glass brilliance; a tiled visiting parlor furnished in aqua plastic and chrome; a steel-grey modern kitchen. Three rectangular wings, each with its own refectory, branched out from this center. Aspirants entered here and spent six months in the postulate and two years in the novitiate before they left the grounds for a juniorate. In my target year, 1963, more than 150 sisters lived in this building. Forty-four of the sixty postulants who had entered in August 1962 became novices in January 1963, bringing the numbers in the novitiate well into the nineties. Since the refectory customs were taught in the novitiate, this wing will be the setting for my description.

In addition to archival and interview sources, my memory is a third source of data. I was a first-year novice there in the Lent of 1963. This was Notre Dame's last pre-Vatican year. Their General Chapter met that summer and modified the rituals of dining.

The Angelus pealed forth from the bell tower, ringing out the good news of Jesus, calling the faithful to prayer. When the bells spoke, movement stopped. On the grounds, in the kitchen, the corridors or the chapel, people and time stood still. The in-house paging system broadcast a series of monotone gongs. It was 6:00 P.M., time for supper, the major meal of the day.

Novices approached their refectory down stairways, along corridors, through swinging doors, each walking at her own pace (within the confines of religious propriety). The first-year (novices) were in the habit but a month and some could be heard approaching. They had not yet perfected the quick gliding step that kept the rosaries from rattling. The mistress stood at the foot of the stairs, where she stayed just long enough to allow the novices to complete their penances inside the refectory.

The refectory was a simple rectangular room, wider than it was deep, walls painted pastel pink, floors tiled in mottled grey. The long wall opposite that of the entrance consisted of a series of windows at ground level whose white drapes were open whenever there was "recreation," talking at table. This was the first Friday in Lent. The drapes were closed.

On the right wall there was a swinging door through which the servers passed with their food. On either side were two grey steel shuttered windows which would be opened at the end of the meal to receive the collected dishes.

The room was filled with parallel rows of grey formica-top tables placed end to end across the width of the space; chairs were set on both sides. Only the first table to the left of the entrance had a chair at the head. This belonged to the novice mistress. When it was occupied no one walked behind it.

The only singular piece of furniture was a small reader's table near the windows, the surface of which was barely large enough to hold an open book and microphone.

Arriving before the supper bell had sounded, a half dozen second-years (novices) lay prostrate in the aisle just inside the door. Each sister had unfastened the common pin that held the tabs of her white plastic bib-shaped cape to her habit and moved the cape around under her veil so it wouldn't crack from the pressure of her body. Kissing the crucifix of her side rosary and tucking it into her pocket, each sister lifted up the hem of the outer layer of her habit (a tightly-gathered black apron) so the inside of that garment would touch the floor. Then each lay face down perpendicular to the tables. It was an awkward position to maintain because the heavy cardboard frame of the horse-shoe shaped bonnet extended as far as the nose, preventing the forehead from touching the floor. Too much pressure on the bonnet would pop the common pins that held it to the white linen headband. Most placed one hand on top of the other, making a support for the forehead, and held that position until the majority of novices had arrived. Upon entering the room the sisters stepped gingerly between the prone bodies, trying not to leave a dusty footprint on any part of the black serge.

Those who had no penances to perform found their places at table by checking the name on the plastic ring at the table setting. (The refectorian moved all napkins one place setting each day, thus rotating the entire company around the fixed place of the mistress.) Once in place they rested their hands on the backs of their chairs and waited.

Most likely another novice would approach, tap the shoulder to gain attention, and say, "Sister, please may I ask prayers." "Certainly, Sister," was the response. Both would then kneel down with hands folded and gaze lowered to continue. She who initiated would say, "Sister, please pray for me that I may grow in the spirit of Blessed Mother Julia, especially in [then she would name three virtues such as simplicity, charity, or generosity that had characterized the life of the foundress]." The other would ask her prayers for one such intention and then stand, extend her foot slightly heel down, toe raised off the floor so the other could kiss it easily. Both feet were kissed in this manner and then positions were reversed.

Gradually the low hum in the room would subside, the rising and the falling actions would draw to a close. All would then face the door and await the mistress's arrival. When she entered they would nod to her, turn back to their places and listen for her voice to begin the grace.

The antiphonal grace alternated between the voice of the mistress (versicle) and the collective voice of the community (response). Her hand made the sign of the cross over the table at "Bless us, O Lord. . . . " Their heads inclined forward at the doxology; otherwise there was no body movement.

V: Bless the Lord.

R: Bless the Lord.

V: The poor shall eat and shall be filled; and they shall praise the Lord that seek Him; and their hearts shall live forever and ever. Glory be . . .

R: As it was in the beginning, is now and ever shall be. Amen.

V: Lord, have mercy on us.

R: Christ, have mercy on us.

V: Lord, have mercy on us. Our Father (silently) . . . And lead us not into temptation.

R: But deliver us from evil. Amen.

V: Let us pray. Bless us, O Lord, and these Thy gifts, which of Thy bounty we are about to receive. Through Christ our Lord.

R: Amen.

Reader: Pray, Lord, a blessing.

Mistress: May the King of everlasting glory bring us to the feast of life eternal. Amen.

The mistress was seated and then the novices. About twenty of the latter were scheduled to kneel on Friday, so each carefully turned her chair sideways and tipped it under the table, sliding it as far as it would go without its touching the novice on the other side. Kneeling at her place each covered her rosary by taking the tip of her apron hem and drawing it over diagonally, tucking that edge into the waistband. The linen napkin was also tucked in at the waist.

Those who were seated kissed the crucifixes of their side rosaries as they placed those rosaries in their laps; then they lifted their aprons from either side, creating a pleat or fold which covered them. The white linen dinner napkin was placed over the whole. While waiting for the food, they again placed their hands on top of each other and rested them on the edge of the table.

The 1553 letter of Saint Ignatius was read, that famous letter on the virtue of obedience urging the renunciation of will and judgment, the one that exhorted the members to obey superiors as one would obey Christ. Those Ignatian ideals were also the foundation of Julie Billiart's dreams, and from the earliest times of the Institute were required table reading.

As the novices listened to the Jesuit vision, they were attentive also to the needs of the table. Servers in white aprons circulated rapidly around the tables placing the common dishes of each course before the mistress and before every group of six people. No one touched a dish at any table until the mistress had placed her portion on her enamelware dinner plate. Without appearing to be watching, novices picked up movement cues from head table and synchronized food distribution.

A small plate holding six half slices of white bread was passed first. Each novice took a piece and put it on the raised edge of her white dinner plate; a small portion would be used to clean the dish between courses and after the last course. Soup, meat or fish, vegetable, canned fruit, or other dessert were all eaten from this one plate. Water and tea were drunk from one bowl. The menu tonight consisted of corn chowder, fishcakes, mashed potato, and green beans from the kitchen; raspberry jello and vanilla cookies from the bakery.

The utensils were used in the same manner as common to American society. The bowls required concentration. Their six-inch mouths were held by the opposing pressure between thumb and third finger, with some assistance from the index finger placed inside the edge.

A wide-angle view would show a pattern of uniform rows of white veils (none of which touch the back of the chair) broken by scattered kneeling figures. Dishes move in a zigzag pattern down the tables and are carried off when empty. Occasionally a seated figure catches the eye of a moving one; then a palm pressed to the table produces bread. A knife pointed downward produces butter; a tapping index finger, salt and pepper; a lifted dish, refill of the original contents.

When food and drink have been distributed and consumed, the mistress taps her empty bowl with a knife, signaling the reader to conclude the passage. As the scrap plate and the silverware tray are passed, seven or eight sisters line up in the aisle to the right of head. In rapid succession they kneel very close to the mistress's chair and softly ask a penance for their imperfections in carrying out some rule or recommendation, which they name. They are assigned rote prayers (Hail Marys, Our Fathers) to say as a penance; some are reprimanded; they kiss the floor and return to their places.

For the last few whispered exchanges the room is in stillness; all the seated novices appear to be wrapped in prayer. The final sister kneels farther away than the others had and projects her nervous voice to fill the room as she says: "Sister [she addresses the mistress by name], I thank you for your goodness to me. I ask pardon for the trouble I have caused you and that of the sisters for the bad example I have given. I ask your prayers, Sister [name], and that of the sisters, that I may begin a new life." No oral response is given. Everyone now knows this is either the sister's baptismal day or her feast day. All stand now for grace.

V: He hath made a remembrance of His wonderful works, being a
   merciful and gracious Lord.

R: He hath given food to them that fear Him.

V: Glory be to the Father . . .

R: As it was in the beginning, is now and ever shall be. Amen.

V: Blessed is God in His gifts and holy in all His works: who lives and reigns world without end.

R: Amen.

V: O praise the Lord, all ye nations; praise Him all ye people.

R: For His mercy is confirmed upon us, and the truth of the Lord remaineth forever.

V: Glory be . . .

R: As it was . . .

V: Lord, have mercy on us.

R: Christ, have mercy on us.

V: Lord, have mercy on us.

R: Our Father . . .

V: And lead us not into temptation.

R: But deliver us from evil.

V: He hath distributed. He hath given to the poor.

R: His justice remaineth for ever and ever.

V: I will bless the Lord at all times.

R: His praise shall be always in my mouth.

V: In the Lord shall my soul be praised.

R: Let the meek hear and rejoice.

V: O, magnify the Lord with me.

R: And let us extol His Name together.

V: Blessed be the name of the Lord.

R: From henceforth now and forever.

V: Vouchsafe, O Lord, for Thy name's sake to reward with eternal life all those that have done us good.

R: Amen.

V: Let us bless the Lord.

R: Thanks be to God.

V: May the souls of the faithful departed, through the mercy of God, rest in peace.

R: Amen.

[In silence each one recites Psalm 129, the "De Profundis" for all the souls in purgatory. The sign of the cross recited in common, begun by the mistress, completes the table prayers.]

The novices remain at their places until the mistress crosses the threshold; then they move quickly to the kitchen, bakery, or scullery. One novice remains at her place. Unable to eat her dinner at the same rate as the others, she must stand to complete her meal.

Ritual Guidelines: Rules, Customs, and Recommendations

The written guidelines for refectory behaviors in Notre Dame state no overarching design, claim no inspirational source, posit no historical indebtedness. Characteristically the documents of the congregation stress the exceptional qualities of their foundress: her faith, vision, and practical achievement. They celebrate Julie Billiart's integrity and autonomy. Since she had no interest in nor made any contribution to theories of spirituality (Linscott 1969: 110), few of her followers have studied the derivative nature of her operative spirituality. In recent years Sr. Julie de la Sainte Famille Chisholm, however, has established the Notre Dame–Jesuit connection. Even though the Society of Jesus was against any attempt to adapt their rule to one for women, it is the Ignatian concept of obedience that is the very lifeblood of Notre Dame's constitutions (Chisholm 1954: 129). In turn, the customs and recommendations that are the content of this present study flow from constitutional ideals.

Julie Billiart, under obedience to Father Varin (her chosen superior and later a provincial in the Society of Jesus) was commanded to keep a written record of all that happened in those early days: a task she delegated to her companion, Francoise Blin de Bourdon. In this command lies the genesis of Notre Dame's penchant for committing everything to writing.

Francoise, known in religion as Mother St. Joseph, not only

drew up the commissioned memoirs but in her capacity as second mother general also wrote the first of many books of recommendations. The 1893 translation has seventy refectory rules. Forty of these concerned table manners, addressing the proper body position at table, the proper interaction with others at table, and the proper manner of consuming the food. Examples are:

Keep your hands on the table and your elbows close to your sides: do not lean back in the chair, nor place your elbows on the table.

Be polite and attentive to those around, but do not urge them to take food, or help them from the dish; do not interfere with what others eat, speak of it, or even notice it.

Do not take a second bite before finishing the first, or make two sips from a spoonful. (Private Rules, SND 1893)

The other thirty could be called acts of religion: attentiveness to prayers, deference to the superior, silence of action, moderation, poverty, good order. Examples of these are:

Make the sign of the Cross with great respect, and do not turn to sit down before finishing it.

Offer water a second time to the Superior. Do not take bread and butter which are near her unless she present them. Avoid passing behind her chair.

Rise and sit without noise.

Eat moderately so as to be neither the first nor the last.

Eat the crumbs that are beside your plate.

Notify the waiter when anything is needed, do not rise to procure it. (Private Rules, SND 1893)

Most of these were still being observed in the 1960s.

Customs and recommendations had very long lives. Theoretically there was a ranked order to the observance of the rules: the gospel first, then the constitutions, followed by the customs and recommendations. If there was an apparent conflict, one would follow the superior text. In practice, however, these distinctions were blurred. Sisters were encouraged to think of every type of rule as a means of sanctification, and disobedience to the same as the road to ruin.

A highly valued 1893 pamphlet entitled *Observance of Rules* and attributed to "a Jesuit" stressed this point. Published by the same press as the *Private Rules*, it has turned up in the company of reprints and pronouncements from prominent ecclesiastics, superiors general, and well-known lecturers. Apparently every house received at least one copy (SND 1984, Letter). A precis of this two-page retreat talk reads:

A Community retains its fervor and its ability to sanctify others by observing its Rules. Other congregations have become lax, lost their primitive spirit, and sadly, but justly, have had to be suppressed by the Pope. Sisters of Notre Dame should experience joy, therefore, when superiors enforce the Rule because conforming to it contributes to the preservation of the Order. All rules are inspired by God and therefore all are important. To distinguish which is more important than another is a fruitless exercise as all are to be obeyed. Without the discipline of the Rule the Institution would be no more than a worldly society, a gaggle of garrulous women. Be duly warned: most infractions against the Rules are sinful, often against the vow. (SND: 1893a).

The sisters relied on their retreat masters to guide them along the path of salvation. The advice they received was ill conceived and legalistic. Insignificant recommendations and gospel mandates were given parity, and the very idea of prioritizing the various rules was branded a temptation.

"We eat without tablecloths, use box-wood spoons and forks and ordinary plates and bowls" (SND 1934c: 8). Attempts to change this recommendation met with emotional resistance because the presence or absence of those particular objects had come to symbolize the poverty of the early members; the continued practice bound past and present in the exercise of the virtue of poverty. The Ohio Province introduced a motion at the Fourth General Chapter held in Namur in 1938 to discontinue their use because wooden implements were "highly unsanitary" and "culturally outdated among even the very poor in the United States," but there was strong opposition to such an idea from all other provinces (SND 1984, Letter). Each province was left free at that time to retain or discard them; only Ohio dropped them. The rest of the Notre Dame world continued to use them until the Chapter of 1951.

Whereas Mother St. Joseph's recommendations stated that Sisters of Notre Dame ate without tablecloths, her refectory customs said they could be used when the reverend mother came to visit. Subsequently tablecloth legislation showed a remarkable development. By 1934 there were seven occasions for their use: on the feast days of the foundress, the superior general, or the local superior; the visit of the superior general or the provincial superior; the centennial of a foundation; a golden jubilee of a profession; or an extraordinary feast. Celebrational status could be achieved, it seems, by rank, age, or holiness.

Most of the refectory customs dealt with group behaviors, whereas most of the recommendations dealt with individual behaviors. The customs also dealt with norms in conflict. They legislated, for example, that when a feast day falls on a fast day the usual feast day recreations were omitted at breakfast and lunch.

Refectory reading was also legislated. The *Imitation of Christ* was held in high regard. Mother St. Joseph ruled that when that text was to be read at dinner, the reader must follow a special ritual—she must kneel to present the book to the superior before beginning her reading.

In 1934 a new list of twenty-three refectory customs and forty-four recommendations was issued. Careful attention was paid to the subject matter for table reading. The featured text at dinnertime was *Christian Perfection* by Rodriguez, the sixteenth-century Jesuit novice master whose instructions on religious life had long been compiled into a classic multivolumed set.

The shorter meal was marked for readings on the lives of the saints, but variations were allowed for liturgical seasons. In Lent, for example, the epistle and gospel of the day were read at dinner and those were followed by selections on the sufferings of Christ. After Easter the Bible selections were taken from church histories. On Sundays and feast days chapters from the fifteenth-century text mentioned above, the *Imitation*, were read before recreation was given. Finally, ten titles were listed which could be interspersed with Rodriguez, but even with all the variations the Jesuit novice master reigned in Notre Dame refectories.

Another concern of the 1934 listing was the uniformity of penitential practices. Formulas for the asking of prayers, the asking of penance, and for the act of reparation were given. The intention seemed to be to safeguard the traditional ways of speaking and enacting them and to specify the occasions when their practice was compulsory.

The refectory penances of that time included three positions for eating (kneeling, standing, sitting on the floor) as well as the practices of begging a meal, kissing feet, and prostrating near the door. In

addition the entire community knelt for meals four times a year—
at supper on Ash Wednesday and Good Friday and at two points
during the annual retreat, confession day and the evening before
vow renewals. On that same evening the retreatants recited the act
of reparation quoted earlier in the description, but they added one
phrase when thanking the superior for her goodness to them,
"particularly for having allowed me to make the retreat."

Reparation was mandated on three more occasions. If a sister
was missioned to a new house she recited the act of reparation at the
last meal before she left for her new assignment, substituting "that
I may accomplish the Will of God in all things" for the phrase "that I
may begin a new life." On the evening before the opening day of
school each year the sisters engaged in that apostolate recited it,
either before grace at meals or at conference. Finally it was said as
a community on New Year's Eve, but not necessarily in the refectory.
Every recitation was followed by kissing the floor.

The only Institute custom that mortified taste was that of eating
dry bread (no butter) on Fridays. The problem must have been
whether or not to observe that practice if another fast day of the
Church had fallen on a weekday in that same week. The solution
given was that dry bread would be eaten on the fast day, not on
Friday. In 1934 there must have been quite a few sisters dispensed
from the fast and there was an obvious desire that all should observe
the same customs universally, so an equivalent mortification was
devised for these members. They were to eat breakfast kneeling,
after which they would extend their arms to recite five Our Fathers
and five Hail Marys, then kiss the floor.

Custom 18 states that "we do not perform corporal penances or
acts of humility on Sundays or feast days." In addition to reinforcing
the connections between liturgical concepts and religious behaviors,
this item provides the terminology in which the members viewed
these actions. It would appear that their proper observance was
significant since they were so highly regulated: sixteen of the twenty-
two refectory customs concerned these "corporal penances and acts
of humility."

The recommendations did not cover formal corporal penances,
but they did attempt to discipline the body. Many table manners of
society include such disciplines and it is not evident which of the
1934 regulations were repetitions of behavior patterns of polite
society and which belonged to the convent proper. In this list the

sisters were reminded not to lean against the chairs, or gesticulate, or keep two hands on the bowl as if to heat them. When the hands were not in use they were to be modestly folded one over the other on the edge of the table (not on the lap). When drinking from the bowl (called a goblet here), the sisters were to keep their eyes cast down.

The subject matter for recommendations continued along the lines established in the nineteenth century: respect for authority, poverty, order. One-fourth of Mother St. Joseph's items were repeated and/or embellished in 1934. The feature, in fact, was the degree of embellishment of the old and the specificity of the new. Reading them suggests that the sisters/authors strongly disapproved of regional as well as individual variation.

In regard to the superior the recommendations state that the sisters turn toward the door by which she is to enter in order to greet her; that they not read while waiting; that they not unfold their napkins, eat, or pass plates until she does; that the reader pause if another speaks to the superior; that one must ask permission to continue eating (through sign) if one is not finished when the superior passes the plates.

The recommendations on poverty were apparently designed to keep the furniture or utensils from being scraped or damaged, dishes from being broken, food from being spoiled. So, for example, sisters were advised to lift the chairs by the back; not to place them against the wall, against the table, or on the table (to clean); not to leave tin spoons in cans of preserved fruit. Item 28 is an example of the high degree of specificity of these rules (The dinner plate had a raised edge and was called a bowl at this time; the container for liquids a goblet.): "When carrying goblets, bowls, etc., do not put the fingers on the rims inside, but hold them by the lower part. Carry at a time only four meat or vegetable plates when of crockery ware; six meat or vegetable plates when enamelled; twelve plates; one pile of six large bowls; two piles of eight goblets; two coffee pots in each hand and two pitchers in each hand. This number may vary according to the kind of dishes." These, like most other regulations, were in effect until the first Chapter of the Vatican II period, the summer of 1963.

Archival records yielded information on what the customs were, how they were enacted, and how frequently they were performed. The latter is key to evaluating the weight given to acts of penance and humility, internally and comparatively. In Notre Dame the following frequency was mandated: on a weekly basis one asked prayers of two sisters, kissed the feet of three sisters, asked table penance twice. On a monthly basis one prostrated once and took supper in penance in three different ways: kneeling, sitting on the floor, kneeling and begging. In the latter situation another person (usually the server) put the food on the penitent's plate, determining what would be eaten and the quantity. This was the norm for most of the year. Sisters could ask for an increase in penances during Lent, on fast days or ember days.

The California archives contain a seven-item list from the then reverend mother, stamp dated 1949, which clarified questions submitted by the mistresses of novices concerning refectory penances. Six items were negative—things that were no longer done; e.g., supper in penance is never taken standing. The positive item reads, "The bracelet should always be worn on the left arm." The "bracelet" resembled a row of interlocking links of a chain link fence. The points of the links put pressure on the arm but did not pierce the skin. Any flexing of the muscles would bring a sharp reminder of its presence. Subject and superior decided on frequency and duration of use. The reason for its being mentioned in a list of refectory items is not apparent, but in presenting a picture of all the physical disciplines imposed during the rituals of dining, it is helpful to realize that some members were using these devices as they ate.

In the 1950s changes in the customs were made in the direction of adopting some of the labor-saving devices, hygienic practices, and habits of society at large. As mentioned earlier, the wooden forks and spoons were discontinued (1951), plastic napkin rings were introduced (1957 "Directives of the General Chapter"), and paper napkins were allowed for visiting sisters. Cloth napkins were laundered more frequently and were placed on the lap instead of being pinned to the collar. Two of the penitential practices were dropped (sitting on the floor, begging) and a greater number of recreations at table were permitted. One directive for the superiors stated that sisters need not kiss the floor when they made a noise at table as they made more noise in so doing. (However, not all of these directives were immediately or universally embraced. In the opening description of the Ipswich novitiate the novices were kissing the floor because that practice continued there.)

In 1957 a new list of materials for table reading was given which gave greater room for choice; instead of prescribed titles or authors, only categories were mentioned. Superiors could select the reading from encyclicals of the pope, pastoral letters from the bishop of the diocese, spiritual articles, "edifying" biographies, and lives of Julie Billiart and Mother St. Joseph.

The 1966 compilation of the 1963 chapter directives ("The Customs and Recommendations of Sisters of Notre Dame") included a one-page introduction that consisted of remarks from two theologians, B. Haring and P. Berg. The latter again stressed the importance of observing the most insignificant custom because all are the patrimony of the religious family. Unlike the anonymous confrere of 1893, however, he also stressed the necessity of having charity as the motive for the practice and of distinguishing the order of the hierarchy: gospel, canon law, constitutions, private rules, book of customs. Father Haring called for adaptation to the times, for continuity and initiative. Analyzing, prioritizing, adapting was the task of this first renewal chapter. The introductory page concluded with an editorial statement which read: "The principal practical modifications will be found in the book of Customs, which, with a view to ensuring a more efficacious apostolate, will differ in certain points from one country to another." Carrying out the mission was identified as the primary value; uniformity of practice gave way to a recognition of cultural diversity. New theological understandings were being applied to every aspect of the sisters' lives, including the rituals of dining.

The superior's liturgical leadership was significantly reduced when the lengthy table grace was replaced by the unison recitation of the familiar "Bless us, O Lord, and these Thy gifts which we are about to receive from Thy bounty, through Christ, Our Lord. Amen." The superior still blessed the table by making the sign of the cross during the recitation and blessed the sisters before breakfast, however. The sisters did not face the doorway while waiting for her, but faced each other. And the superior was permitted, but not required, to practice the same refectory penances as the other sisters. The public penances that took place in the refectory were limited to eating dry bread weekly, kissing the feet of a sister once a week, and taking a meal kneeling once a week. Asking the prayers of the sisters was moved to conference and prostrating was done privately with the permission of the superior.

The decrease in the number of refectory penances was accompanied by an increase in recreations. Conversation was allowed for at least one meal on forty-four occasions in addition to the meals of the fifty-two Sundays of the year. Nothing was said about dishes or tablecloths but in practice convents were allowed to introduce cups and saucers, dinner plates and soup dishes, and eventually table mats or cloths. Notre Dame was no longer marked by boxwood forks and spoons, one plate, one bowl, and the absence of a tablecloth.

Transmitting the Meal Tradition

In 1963 Notre Dame's General Chapter elected its first American mother general. At that time, too, novice mistresses of California and Massachusetts who had held office for twelve years and nine years respectively were replaced by sisters who were then mistresses of juniors or postulant mistresses. Some ten years previously one of these sisters had attended the University of Notre Dame for one of its first Institutes of Spirituality. Other than that educational experience and the positions they held at the time there was no specific job training, nor was any deemed necessary. The provincial and her council had made recommendations to the reverend mother for these appointments but the reasons behind the recommendations were not shared with the appointees.

The initiation into ritual practice for those who entered between 1960 and 1964 reflected the methods of four different mistresses, whose attitudes toward and interpretations of the customs varied greatly.

One of those in office until 1963 remembered that as a novice she had learned the penances by seeing them. From her own liberal arts education she could figure out their possible historical origins, but no such explanation was offered to her. In her day they were told religious life was the world turned upside down: so they took it as it was.

As a mistress there were many things she made the novices do that she personally disapproved, she said, but she did not feel she could tell them that. Instead she read widely and tried to connect the practices to sources in history and liturgy. She recalled that when she would first inform the novices about penances they were alarmed and incredulous. Because she, too, found the practices both repugnant and valueless, she experienced distress in passing them on. She tried to make the transition as easy as possible.

Her counterpart on the other coast experienced no distress in herself and received no complaints or negative reactions from the novices. The job of a novice mistress was "just teaching the life you were living." The customs were a part of that life.

Both of those who assumed the task of novitiate formation in 1963 knew that change was forthcoming. One had been present at the General Chapter in 1963 where the incoming reverend mother had made it known that in her view formal penances were incompatible with American culture and no longer acceptable to the young. In informal conversation elsewhere the newly elected mother general expressed her disapproval at the too rigorous application of the penances that she had observed in some Massachusetts houses.[1] The other appointee did not know this, but the workings of the Vatican Council and the new theologies being published that stressed psychological well-being in religious maturation alerted her to the inevitability of further change.

One of these two new appointees was taught during her own period of formation that the refectory penances were simply customs inherited from Belgium. One mistress whom she had for a brief period did speak of self-annihilation as an interior disposition, but as a novice she had never experienced any such movement in her soul, so she dismissed that type of thinking. She assessed her own life performance in this area as "ritualistic obedience." In passing the customs on to her own novices in the 1960s she explained that the special practices still in effect (asking prayers, asking penance at the end of the meal, kissing feet, kneeling for meals) were customs that assisted the practitioners in developing habits of humility.

Her counterpart in the other province considered the refectory penances unattractive when she first learned them, but she made them meaningful (although she never deemed them essential). She recalled being taught and teaching that humility was basic to the practice of kissing the feet of the sisters and self-annihilation to prostration. Self-annihilation was a death to the selfish, ambitious, or proud aspects of a person. It was opposed to self-aggrandizement (a calling of attention to the self), which violated the virtue of humility. Going against self strengthened the person so that, hypothetically at least, she was prepared to do the difficult thing in life. And in the asceticism of the period prior to Vatican II, she reminded me, what was naturally unattractive was spiritually healthy.

This mistress thinks she also suggested to the novices that they consider how unworthy they were of the greatness of God's love. Although she did not remember this attitude as part of what was transmitted to her, she felt that it was part of her responsibility as a novice mistress to interpret the customs so they meant something to new people. "Things that were sacred to our lives were disappearing," she said, and she wanted to offer as much meaning as possible to the actions that remained. This was her conscious motive even though she was fairly sure that these penances would not be a part of their future. She was in a bind, but she reasoned that the novices would be in a worse bind if they were sent out into communities where the customs were still respected.

This mistress did not remember any novices complaining that these practices were difficult. If they had, she would have encouraged them to do them, as they were part of the life.

My interviews with Notre Dame's post-1960 novices brought memories of all these different approaches to the surface.[2] Three remembered that only the mechanics were demonstrated; four spoke of humility and curbing one's pride; one remembered a historical/ liturgical link; two could not remember. The words chosen by one of the latter were almost identical to those of a Dominican peer who also could not remember: "They were given some kind of meaning but meaning fails me now . . . because they were so foreign."

These novices, however, saw the purposes of the special behaviors in a very different light from the official explanations. They described them variously as outdated holdovers from Europe; daily reminders of belonging to the "club" of religious life; conditioning to "perfect obedience" (the instantaneous execution of the superior's command). A great number argued that the effects the practices had on them provided the best indicator of purpose. They found them humiliating, particularly when kissing the feet of the sisters, asking prayers, and making the act of reparation. The penances were constant reminders of the self-concept that was held up as an ideal: to consider oneself to be the least, lowest, and last in importance in the community. They regarded the penances also as a negation of all that was natural in favor of all that was spiritual, when these are considered to be in conflict. One named them the tools whereby each person's spirit was broken so that she could be remolded in the new corporate image.

The hostility, frustration, and emotional pain was evident not only in these statements but in the interview process as well. The first part of the questionnaire, designed to bring the sisters back in time to their novitiates, to stimulate their recollection of details of place, material objects, frequency and manner of eating, and the penances enacted, often provoked unexpected—and revealing— responses. We frequently interrupted the formal question-and-answer pattern so the respondents could deal with the emotions of their memories.

In one case the sister remembered everything until I asked her to state in which of the penances she took part. They all sounded vaguely familiar, she said, but she could not remember whether she personally had done them or had learned of them some other way. This confusion was very upsetting to her and in the ensuing period of reflection she could recall only the feeling of being "terrorized" whenever she was in the refectory. Until the interview she had not known that she had suppressed this part of her past.

Two of the four sisters who blurted out, "I hated it!" during the review questions were also unable to recite the formulas for asking prayers or for making the act of reparation. They were puzzled over that memory lapse but eventually conjectured that it was too painful for them to recall.

One sister spoke slowly and with great difficulty, trying to hold back the tears. One memory she shared was that for some reason unknown to her at the time, her family rarely came for the full two hours a month allowed for visits. Much later they told her they couldn't bear to witness the personality change that was taking place in her. They grieved the loss of a confident, competent, cheerful daughter who had apparently succumbed to the novitiate training. She had not succumbed internally but was fighting for survival. One technique she and a few friends had devised was to compose and sing lyrics to a "survivor's song," vocalized whenever tensions were high.

In another novitiate another novice successfully discovered her own survival technique. Counting on the large numbers to disguise her action, she stopped doing all the required penances and her absence was never noticed.

Another told me that for a long period of time she was so tense that she involuntarily regurgitated her main meal and could hear that others were doing the same. When asked if she told the mistress, she replied that she reported a nervous stomach but did not go into detail. It was pointless to say more because it was evident that no one could be an exception to taking part in the customs.

Anger was the constant state of another. All of these customs were traps devised by authority to test the subject's continual submission. Time had a value for her and she was furious that time was being frittered away on such useless stuff.

In summary, nine sisters had never integrated these customs into their spirituality. Each had painful memories of the refectory rituals.

One was different. Never having received explanations for what she was doing, she made up a set that was satisfactory to her for the time being. She decided that kissing the feet would symbolize her willingness to be of service; prostration would indicate an attitude of reverence toward God and life (although she could not figure out why the dining room was the appropriate location for this expression). When she was out on mission to the local houses, however, she quickly became disillusioned because it was obvious that the other sisters did not invest the customs with meaning, and the customs depended on mutuality. She discovered at that time also that the formulas for asking prayers kept all of them from genuinely saying what was in their hearts.

In the case of the 1960–64 group, it mattered little what they were taught at instruction. Participation in the actions spoke more loudly than the oral transmission of tradition. The experience produced an inner turmoil for nine of ten candidates.

Among the senior members of the Notre Dame community I discovered a greater variety of memories.[3] Five of them knew of the penitential dining customs before they were officially told of them. Novices were far fewer in the first quarter of the century and the separation between novices and postulants less rigid. As a result two were warned of the customs by novices; another peeked into the novitiate dining room and saw for herself; one was given a Holy Rule by a visiting reverend mother when she was in but a few months (wherein their existence was mentioned but not described). This person was amused that at the end of her postulate the mistress solemnly informed the group of the customs' existence. It was the distinct memory of one that as a postulant she was told not to be frightened or surprised, especially when she saw the sisters stepping over others in the practice of prostration. They were just customs, the mistress said.

Preparing the postulants was not practiced with consistency and there was no period of suspension of the practices when new novices joined the others in the novitiate. Some, therefore, were surprised. In one situation the respondent told me that her whole

band (entrance group) were "such clips" that the mistress thought
they would have to repeat the postulate. She was caught off-guard
when they were passed on into the novitiate, so she forgot to tell
them anything. This particular sister had strong negative reactions
to what she saw. To use her expressions, she thought "she would go
bonkers" the first time she saw someone beg a meal, and when she
saw them kissing each other's feet she thought, "Do I have to lick
someone's boots for my meal?" Another sister who remembered no
preparation said she almost fell over backwards with shock. She was
not upset at the actual practices but with their association with
meals. "Anytime but mealtime," was her reaction.

At the opposite pole were two sisters with very positive reactions.
One of them laughed when remembering this initiation period,
labeling the practice of prostration as "so romantic." Another said
she entered for the difference and "wanted everything." Her facial
expression was one of great joy as she recalled all the customs: she
never had an aversion to any of it. This sister interpreted the vowed
life as a life of consecration that set one apart from others. As a
consecrated woman her goal was to die to self so she could live in
Christ. Taking part in penitential customs, therefore, was a joyful
exercise. Customs of mortification of will and senses were treasured
means of achieving self-surrender. In both of these pairs, representa-
tives of the positive and negative reaction poles, one sister was a
Californian and the other from Massachusetts.

Seven of the ten interviewed said the preparation for the customs did not include any assignment of meaning to them. Two who
did remember said they were told that reparation and penance were
achieved through these practices and that this was their contribution
to the world. Additionally, but secondarily, they instilled humility.

One of the elder members interviewed had herself been a novice
mistress; she had no hesitations about what the customs meant. As
she explained it they were avenues for renewing one's intentionality
and channels of grace. The whole of a vowed life gave glory to God.
The distinctive mark of that life was mortification. Practices of
mortification deliberately and repeatedly embraced by the religious
for the love of God curbed nature and brought graces into one's life
that produced spiritual maturing. To help me understand the concept she compared the process to tending a garden. When one
prunes a tree, she explained, one cuts back on nature for the sake of
the plant. It becomes stronger and bears more fruit. Hers was a

coherent and complete exposition delivered with confidence. The 1914–25 group as a whole, however, lacked this ability to clearly name the purpose of the practices.

Since seven had received no explanation beyond the mechanics of performance, their understanding was intuited from the practices or developed through spiritual reading. One said they needed no meaning: it was sufficient for her that they were a part of the life. Others explained the customs' purpose as mortification, humility, penance, ramparts against worldliness, or indicators of being always on trial—"a vocation is such a high calling that one needs humiliations to be worthy of it."

Six maintained that they successfully integrated these customs into their spirituality (two of these would prefer to be observing them now); four merely endured them. When compared with their younger sisters on whether or not the special behaviors of the refectory became a meaningful part of a sister's life, the responses can be charted as follows:

	Pre-1925	Post-1960
Definite yes	4	0
Qualified yes	2	1
Qualified no	0	0
Definite no	4	9
Unsure	0	0

The table conceals an important aspect of the responses—the contrast of emotional content in the "definite no" entries: the older sisters endured the dining rituals, the younger sisters were enraged by them.

PART TWO

THE ASCETIC HISTORY

3

CHRISTIAN FOOD BELIEFS

In Part One I described the movement patterns of two convent dining rituals, reviewed the archival material that supported those patterns, and reported both the interview data from formation personnel on handing on the traditions and the data from the members on being incorporated into the rituals. In Part Two I move into the history of the Roman Catholic church to explore its food beliefs and customs, especially the practices of restricting food consumption (fast and abstinence). The theological reasons for curtailing sensate satisfaction will be reviewed, with particular attention given to the Dominican and Jesuit ascetic formulations. Once this foundation has been laid, it will be possible to see how the convent food rituals of the Sisters of Notre Dame de Namur were tributaries of the Jesuit mainstream, and why they differed so radically from those of the Dominican Sisters of Mission San Jose, who stood firmly within the tradition of their order.

Dietary Rules

Christianity broke with the Jewish tradition by not imposing dietary rules on its members. Jesus had observed Jewish customs (fasts, feasts, pilgrimages) but had criticized ritual formalism, especially when it took precedence over ethical action. Commenting on dietary rules themselves, he said, "Listen and understand. What goes into the mouth does not make one unclean; it is what comes out of the mouth that makes one unclean" (Matt. 15:11).

The boundary rules and the dietary rules were shattered in one blow in Peter's vision (Acts 10:12–15). According to this account Peter went into a trance wherein he saw a sheet being let down from heaven by its four corners. It contained "every possible sort of animal and bird, walking, crawling or flying ones. A voice then said to him, 'Now, Peter, kill and eat!' But Peter answered, 'Certainly not, Lord; I have never yet eaten anything profane or unclean.' Again, a second time, the voice spoke to him, 'What God has made clean, you have no right to call profane.' " Immediately Peter made the metaphoric connection between food and social boundary. At that very moment when the vision passed, messengers from a Gentile, Cornelius, were waiting to invite Peter to their master's house. Upon arriving he said, "You know it is forbidden for Jews to mix with people of another race and visit them, but God has made it clear to me that I must not call anyone profane or unclean" (Acts 10:28–29). What was startling was the possibility that the good news was to be preached to all and that all were to be baptized, not that the food prohibitions were overturned; but the two went hand in hand.

After Peter received this revelation, Paul interpreted its meaning for the Gentiles: dietary rules, circumcision, and Sabbath observances were superfluous to non-Jews because they were signs of the old covenant. Even though Jesus did not explicitly claim this freedom for his followers, for Paul it was nonetheless a principle of the gospel (Rahner 1981: 84).[1]

In the matter of food Paul taught that each one should be sensitive to the other's conscience. If someone was going to be scandalized by what was about to be eaten, the one whose conscience was most free should refrain from eating it in that company. The kingdom of God, however, "does not mean eating or drinking this or that, it means righteousness and peace and joy brought by the Holy Spirit" (Rom. 14:7).

But what right did people have to kill in order to eat? And what actions transferred the living animal from God's hands to human ones? According to Paul that permission came directly from God, who had revealed that all good things are to be received with thanksgiving. In his first letter to Timothy, Paul warned the faithful of false teachers who would say "marriage is forbidden, and lay down rules about abstaining from foods which God created to be accepted with thanksgiving by all who believe and who know the truth. Everything God has created is good, and no food is to be rejected, provided grace is said for it: the word of God and the prayer make it holy" (4:3–5).

The importance of saying grace before meals is rooted in scripture and tradition, Jewish and Christian. At the Sabbath meal a "berakah" would be recited, beginning with a formula like "Blessed art Thou, O Lord our God, King of the Universe," praising God for bringing food out of the earth. Christians continued those prayers and when the new community moved into the Graeco-Roman world they added another feature from that culture. The pagans sang hymns to their gods and it was believed that "pagan songs had somewhat the same effect as an epiclesis: they were able to summon the demons" (Quasten 1983: 130). So the Christians countered by turning the ancient custom to a new purpose: they maintained the use of hymns, even of solo singing, and they introduced the responsorial forms from worship to the domestic meal in order to summon Christ to the table.

The problems associated with eating were thus resolved, but in the course of time Christianity developed its own food restrictions, limiting the quantity and frequency of food consumption (fasting) and refraining from specific foodstuffs (abstinence). These acts of devotion flowed from ascetic ideals and actively shaped convent food rituals. I begin with an overview of their history and development.

The Christian practice of fasting evolved from the Jewish one. In the Hebrew scriptures fasting expressed a variety of human perceptions: Israel's dependence on God, its unworthiness to receive divine favors, and its repentance for infidelity. At other times fasting was a sign of mourning, of remembering the sufferings in exile. On yet other occasions fasting seemed to add intensity to communal prayers for deliverance from an impending danger (see Deseille 1974: 1165–66). Fasting was undertaken at significant points in Jewish history, such as Moses' fast of forty days on Mount Sinai, but was not obligatory for the entire community except on the Day of Atonement and on the four days commemorating the exile.

The people of the covenant expected their prayers to be heard, their sins to be forgiven, their enemies defeated because God was faithful to Israel. Rites of fasting were oriented around those understandings. In the Christian community fasting retained all its symbolic richness but was oriented around the saving mission of Jesus and the presence of the Holy Spirit.

Jesus, the new Moses and the new Israel, spent forty days in the desert in prayer and fasting. It was a time of choice: three temptations to power that would have subverted the nature of his messianic mission were presented and rejected. Using the text of Deuteronomy for each response, Jesus affirmed that his dependence was on God's power: God alone is life.

Prayer and fasting opened his public ministry, but thereafter the evangelists show Jesus enjoying meals in a variety of homes, sometimes as host, sometimes as guest, always transforming them into sacramentals—human gestures through which he communicated the salvation which comes from God (Rouillard 1982).

The disciples were not known for their ascetic restraint, a point about which Jesus was questioned. There are two distinct aspects to his response: one is that Jesus saw fasting as a form of mourning; the second, and more significant, is that he taught that the appropriateness of that action must be decided in reference to the events of his life, not in reference to the existing Judaic tradition. The passage reads: "Why is it that we and the Pharisees fast, but your disciples do not?" Jesus replied, "Surely the bridegroom's attendants would never think of mourning as long as the bridegroom is still with them? But the time will come for the bridegroom to be taken away from them, and then they will fast" (Matt. 9:14–15).

Evidence from the apostolic church shows that fasting was also compatible with joy. In the exuberant post-Pentecostal period the leaders fasted while they prayed for divine guidance in choosing new missionaries (Acts 13:2–3) and for blessings of the Spirit on their labors (Acts 14:22–23). Fasting was a spontaneous action associated with apostolic decision-making. It intensified the supplication of an already hope-filled prayer.

The *Didache* suggests two other reasons for fasting: as effective prayer for one's enemies (1:3) and as a public sign of conversion prior to baptism (7:4). It also promoted Wednesday and Friday as the days for Christian fasting. This choice connotes mourning, as these were the days when Jesus was betrayed and when he died, and they distinguished the Christian community from the Jewish one, which fasted on Tuesday and Thursday. In the liturgical cycle of the primitive church, weekday fasting and Sunday eucharist were the vehicles for commemorating Christ's passion and resurrection, his work of salvation (Jungmann 1959: 24).

Eventually fasting was ordered into patterned observance; but this happened gradually and at the discretion of local bishops. By the third century most dioceses fasted the two days prior to Easter, not as a sign of mourning but as an intense preparation for the fifty days of celebration extending from Easter to Pentecost, as a physical sign of the expectation of spiritual fulfillment, and as a state of spiritual concentration preceding the reception of eucharist (Deseille: 1169–70).

The tradition of a forty-day period of Lenten fast and abstinence differed from all of the above in that it was ascetic in intention. The amounts of food and the types of food that could legitimately be consumed varied from Constantinople to Rome and from diocese to diocese. Detailed information on the origin and development of the period is not available, but the literature of the fourth and fifth centuries refers to it as a familiar practice, a universal tradition (Schmemann 1974: 136). The ascetic fast consisted of a "drastic reduction of food so that the permanent state of a certain hunger might be lived as a reminder of God and a constant effort to keep our mind on Him" (98).

As Schmemann explains it the theological foundation lies in the biblical connection between the sin of Adam and the redemption by Christ. The first refused to abstain from food and thus succumbed to the wiles of the devil; the second confounded the Tempter during his forty days in the desert by witnessing to the reality that one does not live by bread alone. Because sin is always a mutilation of life, the original sin is presented as an act of eating; but Adam falsely equated food with life. His was a misplaced belief that one could have life in itself as only God knows it. "To be sure, the world was given to him by God as 'food'—as means of life; yet life was meant to be communion with God; it had not only its end but its full content in Him" (94). Therefore the original sin is not confined to Adam. Each one participates in the original sin whenever one looks for life apart from God.

The spiritual benefit of being hungry is that the person realizes the inability to generate life from within, that one is a dependent being and thus must acknowledge the Creator as life. Schmemann views fasting as the only means to recover one's true spiritual nature. The fruits of the effort of redirecting one's physical hunger to a hunger for God are a sense of lightness, concentration, soberness, joy, purity. The Eastern church, he says, sees Lent as a joyful opportunity to enter into the mystery of redemption: there the word "Alleluia" is used as a synonym for Lent (138). By contrast, in the Latin church, that expression of joy is suppressed in the liturgy from Ash Wednesday to the Easter Vigil, an indication of an attitudinal difference.

Communion with God was the goal of prayer and fasting but Christianity is not just a mystical otherworldly religion. Fasting is inseparable from concrete acts of charity toward one's neighbor. The Byzantine liturgy (vespers of the first week of Lent) proclaims: "To your physical fast, brothers, bring a spiritual fast: drop all your unjust actions . . . give bread to the hungry, open your homes to the poor who have no shelter, take upon yourselves the deep sufferings of Christ" (quoted in Deseille: 1173).

Prayer and fasting are a part of Christian asceticism, an approach to life that affirms the cross as the path to resurrection. Jesus had said: "If any one wishes to come after me, let him deny himself and take up his cross and follow me. For whoever would save his life will lose it; and whosoever loses his life for my sake and the gospel's will save it" (Mark 8:34–35). And to the one who asked what must be done to be perfect, he said: "If you wish to be perfect, go and sell what you own and give the money to the poor, and you will have treasure in heaven; then come, follow me" (Matt. 19:21). The asceticism of the gospels is one of loyal discipleship and of detachment from the goods of this life. In the period of persecutions these passages moved many to embrace martyrdom in joyful imitation of their Savior. The blood of the martyrs strengthened the faith of the new church, sparked its evangelistic efforts, and helped confirm its conviction that Christians were "strangers and pilgrims upon earth, that their life was in another and a heavenly Zion" (Chadwick 1958: 14).

The epistles of St. Paul image ascetics as spiritual athletes who discipline themselves to live more fully in obedience to the Spirit of Christ, not just for their own sake but for that of the community. For Paul all the baptized were united in a mystical union and the efforts of each had communal significance (Lachowski 1967: 937–38).

The foundations of religious life as it is known in the Catholic church lie in the counsels of perfection as given by Jesus, as interpreted by Paul, and as enriched by the life experience of the members. Virginity, a spiritual martyrdom, soon became a new ideal of perfection—partially fueled by the apocalyptic expectations. As early as the second century sexual continence, originally valued as an aid to detachment, came to be seen as a condition for the ascetic life. The other features took shape slowly, by trial and error. The task was complex: devising a lifelong path to holiness and wholeness consonant with the New Testament ideals; reverence for life and creation as gift, a willingness to follow Jesus in discipleship and suffering, service of neighbor, poverty, prayer.

In the second century ascetics were not formally organized. Groups of persons who practiced sexual continence met for prayers (though they lived apart), distributed their goods to the poor but did not pool their resources, and wore no distinctive clothing but avoided fashionable elegance (Chadwick: 15). Their work on behalf of local congregations was highly admired; over the century their numbers multiplied substantially and as Christianity became popular, so did the size of their congregations. "As the congregations swelled, and the standards of morality and of worship were inevitably lowered, the contrast between the ascetic groups and the normal congregation became more manifest and their relations more uncomfortable" (16). The fervent looked for alternatives. One possible choice was the solitary life; a form of asceticism popular in Egypt in the third and fourth centuries.

The desert was the remote, austere location for the pursuit of inner perfection, of doing battle with the demons, just as Christ had done battle with the devil during his forty days in the desert. This form of asceticism included permanent continence and external retrenchment in everything the body enjoys: food, sleep, comfortable clothing, and lodging. The desert hermit did not isolate himself completely from the local church but returned to the villages intermittently to preach the love of Christ, to heal the sick, exorcise demons, comfort the grieving.

The most influential theoretician of this spirituality was Evagrius of Ponticus (345–399), a deacon from Constantinople doing penance for an adulterous affair. His teachings reflect Stoic and Neoplatonic ideals and his theological principles were condemned at the Council of Constantinople II in 553; nonetheless his mystical doctrine was very popular and was adopted and disseminated by his disciple, John Cassian, whose *Conferences* became required public reading in monastic refectories for the next fifteen hundred years.

In the theology of beginnings set forth by Evagrius, there existed a oneness of rational beings who knew God; their contemplation of the Divine was deemed essential knowledge. After these beings sinned and were separated from God, their spirits were joined to bodies. Thus, the body was a temporary container for the soul; the resurrection of the body a passing stage; incorporeality was the goal (Refoulé 1967: 644). The journey back to God consisted of two steps—asceticism and contemplation. The purpose of asceticism was to purify the passionate part of the soul, to rid the intellect of sense reactions which are obstacles to contemplation in order to reach "apatheia," a state of inner calm conducive to continuous prayer.

A certain etherealization of Christian life was present in this theology of the desert. Previously perfection consisted in living the virtuous life in imitation of Christ, with prayer as a part of that life. The totality was true worship of God. Now the virtuous life was a basic track leading to the pinnacle of worship as an act of mind (Chadwick: 23). This spirituality led to a contempt for the material world and a preoccupation with self.

Part of that preoccupation with self concerned the systematic elimination of vices.[2] In Evagrius' opinion gluttony and lust were part of the interlocking network of sins and passions that kept the soul from progressing toward contemplation. Continence was the virtue which effected detachment from both of these and from all physical pleasures, enabling a person to refuse "with joy every pleasure of the palate" (Miles 1981: 139).[3] Previously sexual continence had moved from (a) being an aid to detachment (from being invested in the goods of this world) to (b) being a sign of ascetic earnestness, and now to (c) being the control mechanism over all pleasure.

Similar interlocking networks appear in that collection of desert wisdom known as the "Sayings of the Fathers" (Chadwick). Clearly the virtue of celibacy was protected by the practices of fast and abstinence from food, and by silence. Abba Antony advised neophytes to keep their tongues and bellies under control. Evagrius recommended they build a safe harbor against the storms of passion out of a "dry and regular diet, combined with charity" (37). Fasting was also credited with "drying up the channels down which worldly pleasures flow" (56). Significantly, of the seventy sayings on self-control, the powers that are addressed are the powers of the demons, not the power of Jesus Christ.

Not everyone who went into the desert to do battle with the demons emerged victorious from the encounter.

The loneliness of the solitary's life increased the chance of abnormality, eccentricity, even madness. . . . The man whose capital fault was pride or lust or gluttony did not find that he had cured himself by escaping his friends and family. The ordinary aids of the Church—the sacraments, corporate worship—were less accessible. The solitary sometimes lacked wise guidance in ascesis and prayer. The call to self-denial could easily become the exaltation of suffering: ascesis could become an end instead of a means. The movement needed wise organization, wise discipline, wise instruction. (Chadwick: 24)

The need for guidance, for human community, set the wheels of change in motion. Leaders in various areas began to organize ascetics into monastic forms. Pachomius, for example, began his religious life as an anchorite but at his death in 364 was the head of a family of five thousand who had a common Rule and the material goods necessary for this new way of life; a church, refectory, assembly room, cells, enclosure walls (Knowles 1966: 3). The walls are the new boundary. They separated from the general populace those who wished to give radical witness to a conversion of life and provided the members with the privacy necessary for their effort as they conceived it. Behind the walls, Pachomius urged the acquisition of internal solitude and perpetual tranquillity. Chroniclers of his efforts said that everyone maintains "the greatest silence, even when eating their food, so that you would hardly think there was anyone there at the tables where they sit; and although they are gathered together in great numbers, each one conducts himself as if he were alone" (Rousseau 1978: 45). The same description of monastic dining could have been written in the twentieth century.

This second form of religious life and the second type of asceticism are most often dated from Benedict's founding of Monte Cassino in 529, though Pachomius predated this effort by 150 years and Celtic monasticism by seventy-five years (Cada 1979: 2–23). Benedict successfully adapted the ascetic ideal to feudal society; the flexibility and moderation of his Rule made it appealing to many classes throughout the ages.

The discipline of the life included strict obedience to the abbot/abbess, mutual charity, communal ownership of all material items, simplicity in food and clothing, and a daily rhythm alternating manual labor and liturgical worship in an atmosphere of contemplative silence.

Monasticism was a counterculture. It judged the secular world as sinfully oriented toward the false goods of sex, power, and possession. In rejecting instinctual satisfactions the monk witnessed to the belief that God alone can satisfy the human heart and that God alone is the source of life and goodness.

St. Benedict (480–547) was a moderate in his day in the matter of food, but he was of the opinion that an appropriate diet was one that gave the monk the occasion for self-denial and renouncement. It became a rule of thumb that any monastery's fervor could be roughly gauged by its diet (Knowles 1969: 118). It was not until 1335, in fact, that permission was given by Pope Benedict XII for meat to be taken three or four days a week (119), but even then the association between meat and laxity was so strong that the monks ate it by attending a separate refectory in relays.

The life Benedict prescribed was no harder than that of the ordinary person of his time and the abbot had the power to relax the rules, including that of diet, for anyone with special needs. In Benedict's opinion community life as he structured it was one form of the life of renunciation, but not the only form (Chadwick: 27). Cassian's *Conferences* praising the solitary life were read along with the *Rule of St. Basil* condemning the same.

The third ascetic formulation, the focusing of energy, belongs to St. Augustine (354–430). His theories are not always consistent with one another, however: on some occasions he views the body as the helper of the soul, on others as a negative weight (Miles: 146–49).

Sexual incontinence, Augustine's own special problem, was not the fault of his body, he reasoned, but of his dissipated soul. The body, moreover, could condition the soul's learning, and ascetic practices applied to the body could redirect the energies of the soul. He conceived of a person's energies as a closed system; only limited amounts of energy were available to each one and those had to be directed to the soul or they would flow out to the body and to the external world. To achieve this redirection two practices were recommended—continence and fasting.

Fasting, as he expressed it, cheated the flesh to enrich the mind. (In this formulation the body was in competition with the soul.) He wrote: "Why, therefore, is it of benefit to us to abstain somewhat from food and carnal pleasure? The flesh draws one to the earth. The mind tends upwards; it is caught up by love, but it is slowed down by weight" (Miles: 148). Here the "flesh" is no longer a disordered will, but body weight. The contrasting images of rising spirit and earthbound weight fault the body.

Augustine was clear, however, when he stated that the purpose of asceticism was the gathering and focusing of energy on spiritual matters. As quoted in the first chapter, he counseled religious to listen quietly to what was being read in the refectory so that their minds would be strengthened with the Word of God even as their bodies were being refreshed.

Dominican Spirituality

St. Dominic (1171–1221) was heir to all three of the above ascetic formulations and combined aspects of each into the spirituality of his order. He had been a member of the Canons Regular, clergy who undertook a limited parochial ministry, but he wanted to form a mendicant group freed from excessive episcopal restriction who would be both contemplative and active, capable of combatting the heresies of the era.

With the desert fathers Dominic considered the mind to be the highest faculty of the human person. When the mind was centered in God the person was in union with God. According to the Dominican historian William Hinnebusch, contemplation is sought for its own sake, not for the sake of effectively undertaking the apostolate. "The Dominican does not contemplate because he wants to become an apostle. That would make it a means to an end. Contemplation is so superior, that it cannot be subordinated to anything lesser" (1965: 41). This positive valuation of an internalized God-experience made the movement a fertile breeding ground for mystics (Jarrett 1939: 115). The prayer life of saints like Catherine of Siena was nourished here and their visions respected.

Unlike the desert dwellers, Dominic integrated the body into his continuing prayer. He chose to emphasize the positive elements in Augustine's theology, affirming the body as the helper of the soul in focusing the person's energy on the things of God. Dominican prayer affirms the unity of body and soul as a single entity, a substance created by God, belonging to God, one that must be referred back to God.

Both on the subjective side, in its exercises, and on the objective side, in the objects of its devotion, Dominican prayer is an orderly and natural progress from the material to the spiritual world. The liturgy of the Order is full of brisk bodily movement, including an elaborate ritual of inclination, genu-

flections and prostrations, with frequent ceremonial processions from place
to place. Its tradition of vocal prayer is very distinctive; words are so to be
recited and sung that their character as a bodily exercise will not become
lost in meditation and emotion, as is the deliberate tendency of the older
monastic chant. (Reeves 1959: 116)

Dominic's personal prayer was also fully embodied. Gestures,
genuflections, and prostration all had a part, as did vocal prayer and
song. The spoken word was his apostolic medium; he left no written
legacy.[4]

From monasticism Dominic took the asceticism of regular
observance, of community life, of penitential practice. Much of the
rationale for his formulation was Augustinian. Human nature is
disordered through original sin, therefore earnest effort is required
to reorient it to God. Hinnebusch writes: "The monastic observances
help the religious to destroy his vices, leash his emotions and passions,
govern his will, die to self. They attack the self-will and pride that lie
at the root of all evil. By taming the flesh, the observances prepare
the Dominican for contemplation. Whereas the passions entice the
soul from the things of the spirit and focus its attention on the things
of the sense, the observances detach him from material things, and
purify the senses, and remove distractions" (133). The senses were
the enemy of the mind, of "apatheia." Everything was aimed at
closing down the "clamor of the senses," at quieting the "chattering
of imagination" (136).

As a medieval man Dominic was motivated by the desire to help
the souls in purgatory and to participate mystically in the passion of
Christ—ideas unfamiliar to an earlier age. For these ends he willingly
disciplined himself far beyond any requirements of his constitutions,
which stressed not physical mortification but the asceticism of study—
mental activity had replaced manual labor in the horarium.

Reportedly, Dominic dedicated his days to his neighbor and his
nights to God. Hinnebusch records that Dominic used a bed so
infrequently that he never really had one of his own (1965: 31).
Instead he maintained nightly prayer vigils until sleep overcame
him. Then he would doze off wherever he was—in a chair, on the
floor, leaning against an altar. He mortified his flesh with a hair shirt
and iron chain (instruments of mortification introduced by Celtic
monasticism). A chain was discovered fastened about his waist at
his death.

Dominic's penance was not self-centered, but drew its energy from his belief in the power of prayer and penance to effect the well-being of others, to procure grace for the conversion of sinners, to help the suffering souls in purgatory. He deprived himself of sense satisfactions in order to direct and focus his energy on prayer; he then offered his sacrificial prayer for the reparation of sins.

In the foundational period of the Dominican order, the twelfth and thirteenth centuries, religious interests were focused on the end-points of time: death, judgment, the nature of eternal life, the effectiveness of intercessory prayer for the dead. Dominican spirituality retained that otherworldly focus. The ability of the people on earth (the church militant) to alter the fate of the souls in purgatory was a hotly debated topic of the era.

Jacques Le Goff, a scholar of medieval culture, cites the Franciscan theologian Alexander of Hales (1185–1245) as the most important advocate of the belief that pain is potential merit. To the question of whether or not the suffrages of the church were useful to the dead, Alexander answered: "Just as specific pain entails satisfaction for the sin, so the common pain of the universal Church, crying for the sins of dead believers, praying and lamenting for them, is an aid to satisfaction; it does not create satisfaction in itself, but with the pain of the penitent aids in satisfaction, which is the very definition of suffrage. Suffrage is in fact the merit of the church, capable of diminishing the pain of one of its members" (Le Goff 1984: 249). The Dominican Albertus Magnus stressed that the source of all suffrage is love (263), and Hugh of Strasbourg directed the faithful to four forms of suffrage—prayer, fasting, alms, and Mass (266)—but Alexander of Hales' emphasis on pain as potential merit took a firm hold on the minds of the devout as the means to help the church suffering who, when released to paradise, would in turn intervene with God on behalf of the living.

Alexander had also speculated on proportionality (what kinds of sins required what amount of suffrages to shorten one's stay in purgatory), thereby opening the door to mathematical calculations which eventuated in the system of indulgences. The holy souls who appeared in visions were reported to speak precisely of the time elapsed since death, the time served in purgatory, and the future moment when they would enter paradise if their relatives continued their fervent prayers. "Thus there came to be established in the hereafter a variable, measurable, and even more important, manipulable time-scale" (Le Goff: 292).

In the life of the faithful and in the lives of vowed religious in particular, the period just prior to death became intensely important, often dramatic, and highly memorable. The state of the soul at the moment of death determined its fate. Whereas a holy life was the best guarantor of future happiness and the only security in case of sudden demise, a deathbed confession of major or minor sins also ensured a safe passage. In the Dominican order (founded 1216) this concentration on the last moments of life was evidenced in its first chronicles, commissioned by their General Chapter in 1256. In the 1955 English edition of those chronicles there are six topical divisions, the last of which is the "Departure of the Brethren from out This World." Eight aspects are considered: "Of Such as Suffered Death for the Faith, Happy Deaths of the Brethren, Visions at the Hour of Death, Revelations of Their Departure, Punishments for Undue Affections, Deceits Practised by the Devil, Suffrages for the Departed, Miracles after Death." The chronicles of happy deaths had one or more of these elements: the dying man foretells the moment of his passing; he comforts the grieving brothers; his last words are a hymn of praise; women and shepherds at a distance have visions of the holy Brother ascending into heaven with Mary, who tells them his name; the reported visions coincide with the moment of death; relics of the deceased cure all manner of illnesses. They testify to "an almost fantastic love of the marvellous" and to an age "when the walls that shut material life off from the immaterial are more diaphanous" (Jarrett 1955: xiii). At the moment of death there are no barriers of space and time; all the natural laws of the physical world lose their grip and the power of the heavens touches down. The prayer popularized by Bede Jarrett is consistent with this point of view: "And life is eternal and love is immortal, and death is only an horizon, and an horizon is nothing, save the limit of our sight." Dominican piety emphasizes the continuity of life and time.

Fast and abstinence fostered detachment from the things of this world, therefore their practice was taken seriously. Dominican meals were meager and the rules governing them were strict (Hinnebusch 1966: 358–60), but all could be adjusted for those with special needs (the young, the old, or the infirm). According to these regulations no meat was ever served in the refectory, not even to lay servants. When friars were the guests of others they could take foods flavored with meat. From Easter to September 14 the friars had two meals a day, the other half of the year they had only one, except for Sundays. There were more fasts than feasts; the most severe fast was Good Friday, which called for bread and water only.

The beverage varied with the country. England rarely served wine, and in Bologna it was reserved for the sick. But in countries where it was commonly used, deprivation of wine at meals was frequently given as a penance at the Chapter of Faults. Despite the variation in custom, a general restraint in eating and drinking was expected of everybody. To this end the members were instructed to hold the drinking cup in two hands.

These are the historical facts pertaining to eating in Dominican refectories of the thirteenth century. Of equal interest is the manner in which the meals became a part of the liturgical prayer. Through the ritual of the Divine Office the refectory and chapel were integrated into patterns of contemplative silence, expressive gesture, and rhythmic Latin chant. In this context there was no ordinary time but multidimensional events that tapped into memory and stretched into eschatology. The procession to the refectory would begin after an hour (such as vespers) had been chanted in choir. Lines formed in the atrium or the "cloister of the dead," where in medieval times the deceased lay beneath the stones. This was the place St. Dominic chose for his final rest, the place where the De Profundis was recited for the departed members buried beneath the feet of the living who prayed for them. From the thirteenth century to the twentieth, for men and for women, the movement and sound were the same. A lengthy chant preceded the meal and one followed it that began in the refectory but ended in the chapel choir. "Meals are taken within this liturgical framework to remind the religious that every part of their life is dedicated to the glorification of God. Even eating is a duty symbolizing the more sacred duty of nourishing the soul on Divine truth" (Hinnebusch 1965: 86). Nourishment for the soul was provided by the reading. It included selections from the scriptures, seasonal homilies, lives of saints and martyrs, *The Lives of the Brethren*, *The Lives of the Fathers*, *The Dialogues of St. Gregory*, and the familiar *Conferences* of John Cassian.

Dominican asceticism restricts the body for the mind; it engages the senses to quiet the senses. Affirming God as the author and center of all life, it orchestrates a way of being in the world that is focused in contemplation. Fast and abstinence are part of the physical discipline that redirects energy to the soul.

Ignatian Spirituality

The last ascetical tradition to emerge from the medieval world was shaped by Ignatius (Inigo) of Loyola (1491–1556), the founder of the Society of Jesus. The circumstances of his background and conversion account for many elements of his spirituality. For this reason every summary of his life included the names of two books that he read: the first was Ludolph of Saxony's *Life of Christ*, the second the *Golden Legend* by Jacopo de Voragine, a collection of lives of the saints. These epitomized medieval devotional literature, painting a picture of the human Jesus in the crib and on the cross, a Christocentrism Ignatius retained (Ganss 1970: 13).

Prior to his reading, which took place during a period of recuperation from a leg wound suffered in battle, the young Inigo was a "swaggering caballero" (Olin 1974: 4) entranced by chivalry, women, fame, and honor. These two volumes evoked the heroism of another kind to which Inigo also felt attracted—that of a soldier of Christ who conquered the forces of evil by building the kingdom of God on earth. As he mulled over his choice he noted the movements of his soul, sometimes toward consolation and at other times toward desolation. The former, a gift of the Holy Spirit, brought him lightness, joy, sorrow for his past sins, peace; it moved him to see life centered in God and to exercise the virtues of faith, hope, and charity. The second was from an evil one leaving doubt and agitation in its wake, tempting him to seek his own glory in this world. Over a period of time he learned to distinguish the two and thus to freely choose the Spirit of God. This ability to discern lies at the heart of the *Spiritual Exercises* he later wrote. This classic is a handbook for directors of souls, designed to help them guide individuals through a conversion experience eventuating, it is hoped, in a lifelong choice for Christ.

Another effect of Ignatius' particular conversion experience was his deep respect for the power of the written word which "bears perpetual witness," a phrase he used in 1542 when speaking to members of his society on the importance of correspondence (Rahner, H. 1960: 1). Ignatius was not initially highly educated nor was he ever literarily talented, but his beliefs moved him to labor over his letters (seven thousand remain), to dictate his autobiography, and to painstakingly draw up an original set of constitutions.

As his autobiography attests, Ignatius set out to do penance in the ascetic manner of the saints whose lives he read. He also drew his inspiration from those scriptural passages that stressed lowliness and willingness to suffer with Christ. He wanted to be "poor and lowly like the poor and lowly Christ" and to offer him generous service no matter what the cost (Ganss: 23). This viewpoint appeared in both sets of readings and fit into Ignatius' tendency to "stress virtues opposite to vices particularly prevalent and dangerous in his own era, such as poverty against riches, humiliations against excessive love of fame, and humility against pride" (ibid.).

He fasted, disciplined his flesh, put on the rough clothes of a pilgrim, walking barefoot as he begged for his daily bread and his ship's passage to Jerusalem, where he reverenced the holy places. But in the use of ascetic techniques he always submitted his judgment to someone more advanced than he in the spiritual life, usually a confessor. He was just as willing to eat as he was to fast; his aim was to center his life in Christ. Sometimes self-inflicted hardships did not coincide with spiritual progress, he noted, nor were they accompanied by the gift of the Spirit. Eventually Ignatius concluded that external penances were individual matters and they must not take primacy over the mission: to win the world to the cause of Christ. The constitutions of his society state that "in regard to what is exterior the manner of living is ordinary" (Ganss 80). There are no penances of obligation. The individual who wishes to employ such means must have the superior's permission. However, the superior is free to impose penances on a subject. As Evennett expresses it (1970: 75) "Mortification in the bodily sense was no longer a matter of common rule but one of allowable private enterprise strictly controlled, nevertheless, by a sensible and ever-observant authority."

Ignatius' thinking coincides with that of monasticism when he advises in the *Spiritual Exercises* that one's attention should not be on the food or one's enjoyment of it. Instead one should think of spiritual things, eating temperately, at a moderate pace, observing good manners. The model for the above was Christ at the Last Supper—drinking, speaking, looking as he did (Longridge 1919: 145–47).

The way in which Ignatius interpreted the Last Supper influenced his design for Jesuit dining rituals and that of the congregations who drew their inspiration from Jesuit sources. The introduction to the third week of the *Exercises*, in which the meditation occurs, points to Jesus as the model for humility, "not only accepting poverty, contempt, and suffering, but voluntarily choosing and embracing them, as the means of most perfectly glorifying His Father, overcoming the devil and the world, and procuring our salvation" (135). The paschal meal is not considered alone but as a step on the way to the cross. The meditation consists of three points: (1) sending two disciples to prepare the Supper, (2) the arrival at the place, and (3) "how, after having eaten the Paschal Lamb, and supped, He washed their feet, and gave His most Holy Body and Precious Blood to His disciples, and made them a discourse, after Judas had gone out to sell his Lord" (ibid.). As the prayer develops, the exercitant's attention is directed to Jesus' suffering; the desired fruit of the meditation is a voluntary response to walk this same path.

The Tenth Addition of the *Exercises*, wherein fasting is treated, speaks of interior and exterior penance. The latter is seen as a fruit of the former, a chastisement for sins for which one has sincere contrition. Eating moderately, Ignatius states, is considered not penance but temperance. Retrenchment from the moderate intake of food is penance "and the more we retrench, the greater and the better is the penance, provided only health is not injured, and no notable infirmity ensues" (Longridge 73). The same degree of moderation is suggested for retrenchment from suitable sleep. His third penance is the chastisement of the flesh through the use of hair shirts, the use of flagellation with small cords, the wearing of an iron chain. For this the sensation of pain is considered helpful. "What seems to be most suitable and safe in the matter of penance is that the pain should be felt by the flesh and not penetrate to the bones, so that it may give pain, and not cause infirmity" (74).

Penance is a concern of the first week. In the third week of the *Exercises* a new set of rules is given, rules which the editor suggests are useful for life and which seem to form the basis for the later constitutions of the Society of Jesus. One reason Ignatius proposes rules for the use of food is to direct the attention of the retreatant from externals to inner experience, thus preparing the individual for openness to divine inspiration. For this end he suggests abstinence from those items which are so pleasurable that they easily lead to excessive consumption. Meat and delicate foods are among these, bread is not. Drink occupies a middle category: it is recommended that the retreatant learn what is good and useful and abide by that.

The customs of the Jesuit common meal were based on the *Exercises* and on monastic tradition. Eating was usually accompanied by public reading or preaching—some profitable activity ordered to the glory of God, although conversation at meals was occasionally permitted. A common recitation of a blessing before the meal and a thanksgiving after it were required, as were interior and exterior propriety, decorum, and temperance (Ganss: 156). As with Augustine, food for the body was linked to food for the soul. For Ignatius that worked two ways. Article 278 of the Constitutions states that if members miss the assigned time for confessions they "should not be given food for the body until they have taken their spiritual nourishment" (Ganss 162).

Vermeersch develops the few directives on meals into a seven-page footnoted commentary in *Miles Christi Jesu* (1951: 370–76), a book familiar to most Jesuits who entered before Vatican II. Without explicitly intending to do so, he confirms that the meal is a highly charged event for the Christian ascetic; one that offers opportunity to grow in grace and life and one that exposes the diner to temptation. The positive aspects are religious and social. Eating reminds one of the fragility of life and God's loving providence (Matt. 6:26). When the meal is festive and social the action of the host setting forth food and drink is a form of blessing: the host wishes life for his guests, which they trustfully accept. The negative aspect, that of danger, is footnoted to St. Augustine's *Confessions*. Vermeersch states that during a meal the soul becomes the slave of the material: "The healthy body finds in eating a certain pleasure to which the soul is afraid to abandon itself" (371).

Opportunity and danger invest the meal with religious significance. Ritual structures a solution that maximizes the salvific potential of the positive forces and minimizes entrapment in the negative ones. Vermeersch wants each Jesuit to be aware of and attuned to these realities. He writes that eating should be regarded as a necessity of life to be accepted in simplicity and humility, as a pleasure to be controlled, as an occasion to practice patience and charity, as a situation that can be turned to apostolic advantage. To enter into this arena from a position of strength, the Jesuit is urged to develop a set of interior dispositions and a set of exterior conducts.

The interior dispositions, based on biblical injunctions, entail a freedom of soul as to what is eaten, an indifference to quality or quantity, a gratitude to a provident God and by extension to the superior now responsible for the members' health and well-being.

"An animal devours, a man eats" (373). This is the basic distinction between beings controlled by sensuous appetite and those whose intellect and will permit the choice of other competing goods. The exterior manifestations of interior virtue are found in the table manners of a gentleman, one who adapts to accepted custom in every culture to which he is sent. Here is the union of the priestly-aristocratic traditions, a subject researched with sociological insight by Elias (1978).

Table manners are forms of social control. Habits of "courtesy" developed slowly in the medieval period in the courts of secular society from which they derived their name. They blossomed in aristocratic circles, coming to full flower in the nation states.

While warriors in the service of lords and kings protected or extended geographic boundaries, a peaceful, hierarchic, formal code of behavior came into being, imposing restrictions on the physical body (sounds, dress, movements, speech). Religious life, another hierarchic, peaceful, boundary-conscious society, had intersecting interests in the observance of manners. Hugh of St. Victor (d. 1141) was one of the first ecclesiastics to set down precepts for behavior (Elias: 60). Later clerics (especially in eighteenth-century France) popularized the customs of the elite. In the process *civilité* was given a Christian interpretation and the church proved again that it was "one of the most important organs of the downward diffusion of behavioral models" (101).

There is nothing "natural" about table manners and nothing obvious about the purposes of such items as the napkin, spoon, or fork. In the civilizing process, according to Elias, society exerts pressure on individuals to detach themselves from instinctual tendencies, to suppress the pleasure component in certain functions. It moves toward that goal by fostering anxiety about one's actions, teaching that a certain set arouse displeasure, revulsion, or distaste in the observer (142). From the fifteenth to the eighteenth century the number of suppressed actions multiplied rapidly. What were once rules for sophisticated adults became basic child-training in the next century.

Refectory rules in religious houses were designed to restrict sensual satisfaction in the "lower" faculties; therefore the "higher" faculties (intellect and will) had to be continually engaged with the reading. In addition, the level of table manners had to match the sensitivity of the most delicate members so that they would not be distracted by any "vulgar" action, thus breaking their concentration on inner realities.

Ignatius had been a courtier; he expected his followers to observe good manners. It is not surprising, therefore, to find written guidelines in a society that so admired the printed word. Nor is it surprising to find that these guidelines were outdated before they were replaced: their observance had become confused with marks of holiness. The California province, founded from the Italian one, has such a handbook, published in Santa Clara in 1883 (in use in the twentieth century), translated from one in use "from time immemorial" in the Roman novitiate which was the "nursery of so many illustrious men." (The document probably originated in the early seventeenth century.) It clearly illustrates a lower threshold of instinctual repression. Good breeding required that the following behaviors be avoided at table: spitting; wiping one's nose; smelling the meat; tearing off a portion of meat, bread, or fruit with the teeth; lifting the plate to the mouth; using the napkin as a handkerchief; licking the fingers with the tongue; cleaning the knife and fork on the tablecloth (SJ 1883: 25–27). The only directives that differed from the secular documents collected by Elias for the period have specific religious purposes; i.e., to cultivate indifference novices were told not to sit at the same place at table (the opposite of secular society), and to get the attention of the server it was suggested that they strike the glass gently with a knife.

Elias linked the elaboration of table manners and the repression of the instinctual with the growth of hierarchy and heightened consciousness of boundary. Vermeersch connected them to personal boundary, naming them as "the complement of our rules of modesty and chastity" (374), in the same tradition as Evagrius, who spoke of sexual continence as the control for gluttony.

The discipline of the senses was not the only mortification in the Jesuit refectory. Public penances were enacted there as well, giving opportunity for the practice of humility and humiliation, attitudes toward self fostered by Ignatius. According to the Jesuit "Custom Book" of 1960 these penances included: saying the *culpa* (confession of fault), taking one's meal at the small table (which had become kneeling at the standard table), kneeling with extended arms during the grace before and after the meal, kissing the feet of some members of the community, serving at table. In cases of a major infraction of religious discipline, individuals were publicly reprehended at the beginning of the meal (SJ 1960: 38–39).

The asceticism of Jesuits was directed at the inner workings of the person. It involved a vigilant monitoring of the will, the uprooting of vice and the practice of the contrary virtue. Ignatius, like Francis of Assisi (but unlike Dominic), had a false start in life and both Jesuits and Franciscans are "more self-conscious than the Dominicans"; they emphasize the will and its "perilous power of blindly choosing evil, and of darkening the mind and quenching its natural thirst for truth; its need of moral reform as a step to the liberation of the mind" (Reeves: 110). Those formed in the Dominican tradition find this "galling" (Jarrett 1939: 126) but extremely effective. "Examination of conscience, the minutest inspection of thought and word and deed, the severest scrutiny of the motives and intentions of the soul became the new instrument of perfection. Not outwards in praise of God, but inwards with criticism of self, is the direction and temper of the mind's outlook; not the community act of praising God, but the community act of examining self, shows the development of the new piety" (ibid.).

A Comparative Assessment

The Society of Jesus had no need of monastic tonsure, habit, or enclosure. Refusing these forms was more acceptable to Rome than omitting the common recitation of the Divine Office which was twice (temporarily) restored by order of the Pope (Evennett: 74). In the matter of mental prayer Ignatius' teaching was diluted by his successors. Borgia and Aquaviva dropped the distinctions Ignatius had drawn between religious in training and formed religious; consequently they doubled all prayer times and introduced a full hour of continuing mental prayer which became a hallmark of the society, a Jesuit spirituality, not an Ignatian one (Gannon and Traub 1969: 220).

Ignatius did not look to the clock to measure progress in prayer nor did he look to prayer to measure progress in perfection. Instead, he reasoned that since the Spirit of God was active in the world, union with God could be achieved in action. Although he, himself, experienced mystic prayer, he did not encourage his followers to seek it as a goal. Contemplative prayer was to be subordinated and ordered to the active apostolic life.

Ignatius rejected any spirituality that took flight from the world or that rated prayer over action. For him prayer was a means to an end—"the love-inspired execution of all our actions in God" (Gannon and Traub: 162). The ability to "find God in all things" (as Ignatius most frequently expressed it) was the new perfection. In this schema the role of formal prayer and penance is to guide apostolic action, while apostolic action roots formal prayer in reality (167). The world is the salvific arena where the battle between good and evil forces is waged. Through grace and human effort the redemptive action of Christ moves forward, but Ignatius was too aware of "the folly of the cross" to confine his hope to achievement. In seeking to do God's will on earth Ignatian piety was focused on the God who is beyond the world as well as within it (170).

This schema on activity in the world is distinctly different from that of the Dominicans. For them, according to the three-tiered model of action constructed by Thomas Aquinas, the greatest esteem was given to preaching and teaching—the flowering of contemplation. The second level belonged to contemplation in itself, the third to external actions such as care for the sick or the homeless, works which did not directly proceed from contemplation. This model, however, is based on Greek philosophy and in that model the world is not and cannot be a positive force, nor action a graced opportunity. If one was fully formed by contemplation, "involvement with the world (or with concrete activity in the world) could not add anything positive; its only effect was to dilute, to compromise, to corrupt. . . . This image accords well, of course, with the medieval world-picture of history as a waste, a secular desert, a painful interim between the lost Golden Age and the future Kingdom, and of life as a temptation, a threat, a danger—almost anything but an opportunity" (Gannon and Traub: 160). The piety of the Middle Ages stressed the sinful disordering of the world that was only nominally Christian. Theologians like Thomas Aquinas were ambivalent toward it; writers like Thomas à Kempis were disdainful of involvement in it.

Dominican and Jesuit forms of religious life cannot be dichotomized into Weberian ideal types; inner-worldly versus otherworldly, mystic versus ascetic. However if the endpoints of a continuum were the otherworldly mystic and the inner-worldly ascetic, the Jesuits would be closer than the Dominicans to the latter orientation. In each congregation time as history and time as eternity are dynamically interrelated but differently stressed.

One pattern relative to life and time does emerge as one moves from monk to friar to the fully active apostle, that is, a diminishing sensitivity to nature and its cycles, to rhythmic patterns, to embodied prayer.

All celibates are radically removed from human life cycles. Most monks, however, lived in rural locations where many of their number were directly involved in working the land or tending animals, and like farmers anywhere they adjusted their lives to the seasons, to the daylight and the dark. The liturgy of the hours nurtured another sensitivity to the individual and corporate body, to cycles of redemption, to rhythm and repetition.

The Dominican friars replaced manual work with study and located their priories in the new population centers, losing in the process some of the sensitivity to life rhythms while retaining the liturgical ones, continuing to channel their prayer through common gesture and chant.

The Jesuits had no contact with land or with animal husbandry, eschewing life in common, monastic observance, the liturgy of the hours, and retaining embodied practices only in penitential forms. In their quest for holiness their stress on the disciplined will overshadowed all else. Their particular ritual forms left little room for incarnate expressions of joy, thanksgiving, or reverence for life or creation.

I have observed that Jesuit authors were proud of their break with monasticism—of taking activity in this world more seriously than their predecessors. In their view release from communal obligations made it possible for them to model their lives more closely on that of Jesus and the disciples. I would add, however, that because Jesuits were still part of the postbiblical Christian ascetic tradition which was laden with dualistic concepts, they were not present to this world—to nature or to human relationships—in the manner of their Teacher. The Society of Jesus recovered the world of action as graced opportunity, but was just as ambivalent as its predecessors about the value of the world of creation. Involved as they later became with cultural and political pursuits, they yet remained aloof from the flesh of things. The *Exercises* were a precious tool by means of which Jesuits operated instrumentally on the interior realities of psyche and spirit to evoke the fundamental option for salvation, but their concentration on that arena, their dualistic inheritance, and their disinterest in community distanced them from embodied truths.

Dominicans, in my assessment, were equally concerned with the salvation of humankind, but gave more weight to the power of prayer to effect that saving grace. In terms of embodiment they, too, were ambivalent, but through the daily ritualized recitation of the Office they engaged the Divinity with their humanity and thus retained one form of witness to incarnate grace.

One task of modern theologians has been to retrieve the good news of the incarnation. Creation-centered authors have reminded the faithful that this earth, embodied life, and all flesh are sacramental by virtue of the incarnation; that "we have not been placed in this world and in this flesh in order that we may work our way out; we have been placed in this world and in these bodies because this is where God dwells" (Baur 1983: 254).

Ascetic formulations of Christian food beliefs were variations within one tradition. In that tradition Christians monitored their exterior passions and interior dispositions with an eye toward growing in the likeness of their crucified Lord—his love, his prayer, his service of neighbor, his abandonment to God's will, and his willingness to lay down his life in witness to the truth. Religious families (e.g., Benedictine, Carthusian, Dominican, Jesuit) were closely related in that all members were responding to the invitation to follow Jesus, yet they differed dramatically in the way in which they structured their response to that invitation, giving widely varying weights to the place of action and contemplation, internal and external ministry, and retrenchment from physical comfort in food, clothing, and lodging.

When new congregations emerged, they borrowed their basic Rule from one or more of the well-established families. I turn now to the women's communities whose food rituals were described in Chapter 1 to explore the roots of those rituals, their place in the ascetic constellation.

4

FOOD AND GRACE: NOTRE DAME

Julie Billiart (1751–1816), a founder of the congregation of Notre Dame de Namur (est. 1804), was born and raised in the household of a small shopkeeper in the village of Cuvilly, France. As a young girl, after her family met financial reversals, Julie worked in the fields and later took an active role in marketing the merchandise until her health began to fail in 1774. Difficulty in walking led to paralysis in 1782—a persistent condition for the next twenty-two years. Her paralysis was interpreted as a blessing by the devout, for in the medieval theology adopted by the church, the suffering were an elect, a source of power for the living and the dead. They were privileged to enter into the passion of Jesus Christ and were able, through his merits, to offer up their suffering for the purposes of redemption. Julie Billiart was so chosen and during this period she gave religious counsel to those who sought it. Eventually, "hearing that many clerics, as well as laics, resorted to this obscure person for advice" (SND 1891: 6), the bishop considered it his duty to investigate her activities. She was brought to him and examined for two hours by his theologians, who determined that her prayer was rich and her doctrine sound; and that she should be encouraged to continue her activities. One of the women she counseled was Francoise Blin de Bourdon, a well-educated noblewoman who became her constant companion and who would later succeed her as the head of the congregation. Both came close to being killed as enemies of the state in revolutionary France.

Although they were spared the fate of family members and friends who died at the guillotine, they were as willing as any of their contemporaries to give their lives for the faith. Steeped in the spirituality of the *Imitation of Christ*, they saw life as an exile from a heavenly home. The purpose of earthly life, Julie Billiart wrote to Francoise Blin in February 1796, was the opportunity to grow in God's love, to accomplish God's designs, and to "die completely to ourselves" before being called home to eternity (Rosner and Tinsley, eds. 1974: 58). They passed on that spirit to future members of the Institute.

The idea of founding a religious order grew slowly. In 1794 the two women were introduced to Father Antoine Thomas, a doctor of the Sorbonne who became their spiritual director, drew up a rule of life for them that encouraged acts of charity, and during a renewed period of persecution of nonjuring clergy that began in 1799, joined them in hiding in Bettencourt, where for four years they taught religious doctrine to the village folk. In 1801 Father Thomas was recruited by Joseph Varin to join the Society of the Sacred Heart of Jesus, a group of men attempting to live in the Jesuit spirit during the period of its suppression (1764–1814 in France). Varin, a man who had received minor orders at St. Sulpice and then served two years as an officer battling the revolutionary forces, was instrumental in the founding of numerous congregations of women in this period: the first was the Society of the Sacred Heart under Madeleine Sophie Barat, the second was Notre Dame under Marie Rose Julie Billiart. He later became a provincial in the reconstituted Jesuit Society, but many consider his most enduring accomplishment the spiritual direction of women founders. He was militant, vigorous, and cheerful and urged all he directed to likewise be courageous and confident (Maguire 1967: 540; Godfrey 1975: 286–90).

Father Varin gave Julie Billiart a formal order to undertake the education of youth (Clare 1909: 84) and he encouraged her to think beyond diocesan structures in so doing. Recognizing her intellectual and spiritual gifts, he left her free to find her own spirit for the congregation, one based on her charism and one responsive to the times. She began with the Rule of Mary Ward that he gave her and added features from Notre Dame de Bordeaux (both of these were Jesuit-inspired and suppressed), but she also included items from the Benedictine way of life (Chisholm: 112ff.). In keeping with the egalitarian spirit of postrevolutionary France, Julie Billiart decided that her congregation would have members of one class only (eliminating choir sister/lay sister distinctions), and, envisioning a wide arena for educational endeavors, opted for government under one mother general who could assign members to any house of the congregation without consulting bishops or pastors.

The Holy See had resisted such innovations in the past, being wary of women in simple vows living outside a strict cloister. It desperately wanted to regain its foothold in Napoleonic Europe, however, and saw that these new congregations were well-suited for the times and for their common purpose (Jedin and Dolin: 216), therefore it adapted canon law to suit this new role for women, giving final approval to Notre Dame's Rule in 1818, two years after Julie Billiart died.

The relationship between Sisters of Notre Dame and those in holy orders is complex. In common with the Dominicans and other religious of either sex, there was a commitment to being loyal to Rome, obedient to the pope and the magisterium, and of one mind with the church. The operative theory of grace that supported that commitment concerned structural charism. It argued that the grace given to St. Peter to guide the church was passed down not only to the bishops and popes but to all who held any office of responsibility for the spiritual well-being of others. Informally this was called the "grace of office"; it became effective immediately upon the individual's succession or election to office. Most of those who had this grace were men, but members of women's religious congregations (mothers general and novice mistresses) were thought to be the beneficiaries of this special guidance as well.

In the hierarchy of grace whoever had the greater responsibility had the greater grace. In this model the individual received power to operate faithfully and well from an outside source; effectiveness did not solely depend on natural gifts or talents. Wisdom came from the Spirit.

One result was an increased confidence in the ability to discharge one's duties without consultation with peers or inferiors. In fact, to do so could indicate a weak faith. Since men were the pastors of the faith community, they had no need to consult their flock. Clerics rarely consulted sisters on matters of governance, but sisters always consulted clerics. When women governed large communities of vowed members, however, the grace of office anchored their claim to equality in the spiritual order that safeguarded their independence.

Although she headed the new congregation, Mère Julie placed herself under obedience to priests for spiritual direction. Fathers Varin and Thomas moved on and left others of lesser spiritual

stature as ecclesiastical superiors, confessors, and spiritual directors.[1]
When Father Enfantin was her director, he considered it his duty to
humiliate her so she would be purified from any taint of pride, to
crucify her "nature in its every fibre . . . with a view to counter-
balancing the favors she had received from heaven" (Godfrey: 96).
Knowing that she had a sensitive stomach and could not eat beans
or raw vegetables or drink cold water without pain, he included
those items in her diet, sometimes adding ashes to the water. Francoise
Blin recorded the treatment thus:

Now and then he had her take her meals in the refectory, kneeling in the
presence of the sisters, and without warning he would dash a glass of cold
water in her face; this was done half in jest, half in earnest. His manner of
speaking to her was invariably severe and harsh, even contemptuous—and
this in the presence of the other sisters. At times he would create a scene that
made the community tremble, over some slight or would-be fault of Mère
Julie. He would address her with such contempt that the sisters were taken
aback, even though he had beforehand assured them that he was doing all
this to try her virtue and increase her perfection; in her absence he spoke of
her with the greatest respect. (Godfrey: 144)

Mère Julie accepted this treatment, according to Francoise Blin,
because she believed God permitted it and she could do penance by
enduring it. She also credited Father Enfantin with good intentions.
    Mère Julie shared certain assumptions and orientations other
than those Francoise Blin recorded that permitted her to acquiesce in
the treatment she received. The first was her devotion to the cross. A
woman whom Julie Billiart directed a decade earlier wrote in her
journal that Mère Julie repeated over and over that perfection depended
on the cross, that one must expect to "lead a dying life, that a Spouse
of Jesus Christ had no other pledge of His love than crosses,
contradictions, humiliations" (Clare: 75). Another feature of her
spirituality was the supposition that nature is opposed to grace and
therefore the body to spirit. Nature, as Mère Julie conceived it,
tended to self-satisfaction and inertia, while grace was the source of
energy and activity. When urging her sisters to emulate the Jesuits
for their energy and zeal and for looking at what had yet to be done
for the cause of Christ instead of looking backward at their accomplishments, she would say, "Down with nature, up with grace!"
(Clare: 485). (Whereas the nature/grace dichotomy was a spiritual
reality that was gender-free in Julie Billiart's mind, it was gender-

specific to many of her clerical contemporaries, who frequently identified nature and sinful weakness with the female sex.) The third basis for acquiescence was the traditional Roman Catholic teaching on grace that affirmed the working of the Holy Spirit through imperfect individuals to accomplish some salutary effect in others. She had reason to believe that Enfantin was such an instrument of grace because it was at the conclusion of a retreat with him that he ordered her to walk and she was able to do so.[2]

Over the years Mère Julie learned to temper her natural deference to clerics and to discern their motivations when they offered her advice or disapproved of her decisions. One cleric tried to keep the sisters in the service of his parish while forcing Mère Julie to move elsewhere. The arguments he used were couched in terms of nature and grace, ignorance and enlightenment. Predictably, he told a young sister that listening to Mère Julie was listening to nature. Mère Julie was deceived, he said, but he had light and grace. The one being addressed, Sister Ciska, was not impressed and refused to go to confession to him, despite his constant urging to do so. For this independent stance she was brought before the bishop, who again chided her for not knowing her catechism where one learned obedience to pastors (Godfrey: 70).

Sister Ciska was not the only one to feel the displeasure of the clergy. The vicar general wrote to Françoise Blin thus:

Sister Julie thinks of herself as one sent from heaven to form a religious congregation and to govern it according to her own will. Where are the marks of this heavenly mission? When did God ever say to a woman, "You shall found a religious order, you shall rule over it as you please, you shall listen to no one, neither bishop nor confessor, unless they be reasonable enough to enter into your views. I give you absolute power over the young people who rally under your banner; whatever you do will be done?" . . . But, Madam, the sacred hierarchy, the bishops of the Church, are instruments of God's authority in spiritual things. It is God's will that the faithful obey their pastors; to the bishops he has declared, "He who hears you, hears me; he who despises you despises me." (Godfrey: 87)

None of their arguments succeeded in dividing these sisters from the foundress.

This deep-seated fear of powerful women surfaced in many situations. On a few occasions Mère Julie had addressed the novices when they received the habit, but this behavior shocked some who observed it and outraged the vicar general, who accused her of unauthorized preaching. She stopped this practice as soon as she heard that some were scandalized by it (Godfrey: 91).

On other occasions confessors or ecclesiastical superiors tried to block Mère Julie's journeys to supervise her houses. When Varin became aware of this he cautioned her about giving over her authority and suggested she learn to consult priests as friends without appearing to be asking their permission (Godfrey: 19). But Julie Billiart had been formed in childhood by priests who were both holy and wise, so it was with reluctance and regret that she recognized that some would abuse her trust to position themselves at the head of the Institute, to subvert what God had worked through her to their own ends and for their own power. Eventually Julie learned to trust her own charism; to recall "the counsels she had already received, rather than seek further direction" (209). Francoise Blin de Bourdon evidently made this transition more quickly. Her loyalty was to Mère Julie: in the words of her *Memoirs* any priest who contradicted her was "interfering" and "probably inspired by Satan" (12).

In order to claim her own authority in spiritual matters, Julie Billiart had to learn how to operate within the conflicting claims of the Roman Catholic prestige system, which both honors women and subordinates them to men. A prestige system "defines the ultimate goals and purposes of life for actors in that society. It defines what men and women are, as well as what they are (or should be) trying to accomplish or to become, and it defines how they can and cannot go about that project." It orders "human relations into patterns of deference and condescension, respect and disregard, and in many cases command and obedience" (Ortner and Whitehead 1981: 360,14). Within the Roman Catholic system there is one ultimate goal, sanctity, a state of being that is equally available to men and women because both are made in the image of God, both are redeemed in Christ Jesus, both are instruments for bringing the reign of God to earth, both are to be judged by the same criteria on the Last Day. The belief in spiritual equality was not reflected in the structures for the temporal order, however. Nor was identity of roles ever taken seriously as an ideal historical condition.

Julie Billiart accepted the patriarchy of her era, respected the office of pastor and bishop, deferred to their authority in matters of faith and order; but the control of the Institute was another matter.

The foundation of an apostolic congregation was a God-given trust for which she was responsible and her primary obedience was to that charism. In this matter she refused to be manipulated or intimidated by the men and women who opposed her. She learned how to be political, how to maneuver the system that held consecrated virgins and the teaching of Christian doctrine in high regard in order to protect her sisters and their common mission.

In matters of spirituality, Notre Dame was indebted to a Jesuit theology of prayer in action. Although the sisters' ability to interact with members of the secular society was severely restricted, Notre Dame still shared the goal of influencing time and history by claiming this world for Christ. However, the Jesuits did not want to be responsible for any woman's congregation; nor did Notre Dame want to be restricted to their ministrations. In her long term of office as the second mother general, Francoise Blin de Bourdon (Mother St. Joseph) defended and nurtured the unique spirit and charism of Julie Billiart, unequivocally maintaining the right of Notre Dame to guide its own destiny.

In regard to the proper use of food, Julie's first thoughts as head of the Institute were on supplying enough staples to feed the sisters and the boarders. Her queries to distant convents concerned their gardens and their potatoes. It is true that her Jesuit biographer James Clare wrote: "In the community, fervour and self-abnegation grew apace. Extreme poverty reigned in the house. The food was that of the very poor: for breakfast, dry bread and water; for dinner, soup and a dish of vegetables, except on Sundays when there was a little meat" (128). This menu, however, and the sisters' restraint were the products of circumstance, of limited supplies that had to be stretched as far as possible. Mère Julie needed healthy workers: a good appetite was a sign of a good vocation. There were to be no fasts in Notre Dame other than the fasts of the church as a whole.

In terms of her own asceticism food had never been a temptation to sensual self-indulgence. This was not a result of any cultivated virtue, she maintained, but because of a natural repugnance stemming from her poor health. Eating was a duty. Capable of digesting only very plain food, she had little appetite in the best of circumstances and none at all when faced with a lavishly set table in the homes of the wealthy or when surrounded by coarse and blasphemous conversations at the common tables of inns (Clare: 135).

When her travels forced her to eat on the road, she tried to eat by herself, but her preference for herself and her rule for the sisters was that they eat their simple meals in the convents (124).

Julie Billiart's thinking about food, including the proper place and manner of its consumption, was in line with Jesuit practice before the suppression. In the course of their ministry the Jesuits frequently mingled with the laity but they were nonetheless forbidden to accept anything to eat or drink from them. With typical Jesuit specificity every possible location for such eating or drinking was spelled out. They were forbidden to eat in a town or a fortified town, at country houses, chateaux, in villages, or outdoors in gardens (*Consuetudines Provinciae Germaniae Superioris Soc. Jesu*, 1693 [SND 1983], chapter 4). Many of the penances used by Notre Dame were variations of their practices. The *Consuetudines* (item 2) records the Jesuit refectory penances of the period:

. . . to take nourishment standing at the table, or seated on the floor, or at a little table; to beg for food, bread and drink; to kiss the feet or the floor. However, it is not customary to kiss the feet of those who are seated either at the little table or on the floor, or to beg from these bread or drink.

Food is brought, after the others, to those who are doing penance. But the little table must always be set up, except for the very solemn feasts of Christ and of the Blessed Virgin Mary, of Saints Ignatius and Xavier, and on feasts for the renewal of vows and the dedication of the Church: on these days it is not prepared either at dinner or at supper, or when guests from outside are present. On Sundays and on feast days when the Brothers have the obligation of Communion, we do not prostrate at dinner.

The Society of Jesus and the congregation of Notre Dame de Namur shared a common constellation of refectory customs—doing penance by eating in a variety of uncomfortable positions and practicing humility by prostrating, kissing the feet, kissing the floor, begging food. All of the above were silent actions, but ritual speech was ordered to the same ends, especially self-accusation.

The Chapter of Faults (the public confession of external failure in keeping the Rule) was part of the tradition of all monastic orders in the West from its Pachomian origins through the Reformation Institutes. According to their sixteenth-century custom books, the Jesuits required it formally only for novices (monthly) and scholastics (semiannually) (Schmitz 1953: 488). While it is true they modified the practice, they did not minimize its importance; in fact they expanded the concept. One method they used was the account of conscience—a report rendered orally to the superior on one's right relation to God (prayer, virtue, temptation), community, and mission. Other aspects of the chapter were merely moved into the refectory. There the Jesuits took turns kneeling with arms extended during the grace before meals, after which they recited a memorized formula (a "culpa") which ended with their naming their precise failing. Whereas older communities practiced "proclamation" whereby one made known the fault of another to the assembled chapter, the Jesuits were proclaimed for serious faults by their superior in the refectory and their penalty was made known also. An additional practice that evolved for all classes in the Society of Jesus was the compilation of lists of one another's faults. The three cited most frequently for each member were read aloud in the refectory semiannually.

Julie Billiart held the Chapter of Faults (also called conference) outside of mealtimes, but retained the refectory accusation also, adjusting it so that only the superior heard the individual's failings. The only full-voiced confession of unworthiness was the Act of Reparation (quoted in the opening chapter) which was mandated for refectory recitation on the eve of one's baptismal day or feast day. Theologically it spoke of human beings in original sin, of people who are imperfect by nature, who need to ask for forgiveness from the community repeatedly, and who need to ask for communal prayers in order to live by grace. Out of this spirituality Julie Billiart lived and died; for it was on her deathbed that she turned to Francoise Blin and asked her pardon for the trouble she had given her, though (as Francoise adds) she had never caused her any trouble at all (Godfrey: 204).

Contemporary Responses to the Tradition

In the novitiates of the 1960s in the United States, candidates no longer thought in Julie Billiart's ascetical framework. They did not understand the origins of refectory customs; they were mystified by the anti-body attitudes they implied; they executed them out of necessity without owning them interiorly.

Nine of the ten Sisters of Notre Dame who entered between 1960 and 1964 stated that the special behaviors of the refectory did not become a meaningful part of their spirituality. The tenth said they were meaningful only during her novitiate. All ten answered the question, "Did your founder initiate these practices?" in the negative. Some were appalled at the very possibility, responding in such phrases as, "I would be hard-pressed to believe it!" or "I certainly hope not!" Others, after answering "No," looked at me and asked, "She didn't, did she?" They did not want Julie to be connected to experiences they had found painful and confusing. They preferred to assume that her successors introduced them.

In the pre-1925 entrance group the six sisters who answered that the refectory behaviors did become a part of their spirituality were also of the opinion that Julie Billiart initiated their use. The other four said either that they didn't know (two), that they didn't think so (one), or that she probably did but it must have been forced on her (one). The consistency of response between questions 14 and 15 was entirely unexpected. Those who found refectory rituals beneficial credited them to the founder; those who suffered from them refused to hold her responsible for them.

Table reading, ideally, drew the attention from taste to hearing, shifting the attention from sensual satisfaction to intellectual and spiritual nourishment. Question 19, "In actual practice was the focus of your attention during a meal on your penance, your food, your neighbor, or the reading?" tested whether or not it accomplished its purpose.

Of those who entered in the early 1960s, half rejected the categories of my question. Their attention was drawn to one place, they said, their fear. Some said they were most aware of being "watched" by the mistress; one was trying to avoid making noise so she wouldn't have to kiss the floor; another was trying to swallow her food quickly so she wouldn't have to eat her meal standing after everyone else had left. In the remaining half, three said they listened to the reading unless it was their night for penance; one always had her mind on the penances; and the last had her attention on the reading.

In the pre-1925 group, six said they always listened to the reading. One said she daydreamed. The other three answered that they had split their attention: between reading and penance, reading and neighbor, penance and food.

5

FOOD AND GRACE: DOMINICANS

Mary Backes (1852–1925), known in religion as Mother Pia, founder of the Congregation of the Queen of the Holy Rosary, was five years old when her family emigrated from Neukirchen, Germany, to Philadelphia. She was educated by the School Sisters of Notre Dame in that city and by the Dominican Sisters at Holy Cross Convent when the family moved on to Brooklyn. In her seventeenth year she decided to join the School Sisters but acceded to her mother's wishes to remain close by, entering the Dominican community instead. The formation she received was part of an unbroken chain that linked her to thirteenth-century Beguines in Ratisbon.

The Dominican friars had made a foundation in Ratisbon in 1230 and within three years had organized the nucleus of a contemplative community from among the Beguines who lived in the western part of the city. In so doing they were following in the steps of St. Dominic, who so prized prayer and penance that he framed the constitutions of contemplative nuns in Prouille, France, in 1206, a year before he began his own work of mendicant preaching.

The whole Dominican family consists of three orders which complement and complete each other (Kohler 1937: 14). Each has a different task and therefore a different orientation and organization. The first order, open only to men, comprises clerics and laybrothers and defines its task as the conversion of heretics.[1] The second is composed of cloistered women (choir and lay) whose work is contemplation. The holiness of their ascetic lives is considered to be effective in the order of grace, bringing a blessing to the world and to the labors of the friars. The third order, a product of the twelfth-century penitential movement, is open to laity of either sex who seek a life of perfection; its expression may lie in any good work.[2]

In the first half of the thirteenth century Dominican friars willingly became the confessors, teachers, preachers, and temporal administrators for the contemplative nuns. Convents for women mushroomed under this arrangement and soon the friars realized that the work of the first order was becoming the maintenance of the second. Both the men and women petitioned the pope: the women pleaded for the services that were promised them; the men to be released from the same. In 1267 Pope Clement IV laid down the terms of the compromise: the men were relieved of their fiscal responsibility but retained a limited spiritual jurisdiction (Hinnebusch 1966: 392).[3]

The Ratisbon community was not cloistered in its new buildings until after enough financial backing was obtained to make permanent enclosure possible. In 1237 Count Henry of Ortenburg presented the nuns with such an income—the parish of Schwarzhofen together with all its titles, tithes, and privileges. In return the nuns offered their suffrages for their benefactors. They have done so for the last seven centuries. This foundation is the oldest Dominican women's convent in continued existence. It has survived famine, plague, war, national reorganization, religious persecution during the Protestant Reformation and civil attempts at secularization (Kohler: 20–30).

Events of the early nineteenth century wrought external and internal confusion in the lives of the nuns. Following the edicts of secularization, church property was ceded to princes and lords who confiscated whatever could be sold and dispersed the members of the religious communities. The Dominican friars suffered this fate in 1803, terminating their presence in this city. In that same year the nuns' convent was turned over to Prince-Bishop Dalberg (appointed as such by Napoleon), who demanded that they teach school if they wished to continue as a community. They were forced to choose between returning to their homes and undertaking a foreign manner of living their vowed life. After ascertaining that they could receive special permission to retain their second-order status while thus engaged, they chose survival by choosing to teach. For these women in these circumstances, entering the active apostolate was an act of oppression.

In 1809 the convent stood in the line of fire between the Austrian and Napoleonic armies: a battle immortalized by Robert Browning's "Incident at a French Camp." One-fourth of the town was demolished but the Dominican convent survived the attack.

They opened their doors to the Franciscan women left homeless and melded their communal living for the next three years.

No one knew any longer what regular observance meant. Over the next two decades the discipline of the house became lax, the spirit of penance and prayer diminished. Instead the nuns became enmeshed in relationships of reciprocity with secular society, violating cloister by entertaining visitors in the refectory, violating poverty by giving and receiving presents (Kohler: 50). This was an inversion of right order, for the coins of value for contemplative nuns are never material nor is their arena for exchange in this world. An anonymous second-order Dominican in the Ratisbon line of descent (quoted in Crawford 1938: 303) presents the ideal. She speaks of acts of self-denial (the interruption of sleep for a nightly two-hour vigil, the long fast, and continual abstinence) as "beloved treasures—coins wherewith one may purchase the faltering souls of those who have fallen, or are falling, into sin." Theologically, she continues, her life is an expanded and concentrated act of reparation, an act which in some degree is required of all Christians either for themselves or for others. "On this principle is founded the Communion of Saints, and in the light of such teaching the Dominican nun finds her greatest consolation. She has left the world not because she did not find it pleasant but because without it she can be of more value to other people." Acts of prayer and penance fill the treasury of the contemplative. Herein lies her wealth, value, and well-being.

The reform and renewal of communal life as well as a paradigmatic shift in attitude to the apostolate were accomplished under the leadership of Mother Benedicta Bauer, prioress from 1845–58. When she entered Ratisbon, the community had been "encumbered" (Kohler: 42) by teaching for sixteen years. The young Sister Benedicta, gifted intellectually and musically, flourished in the classroom. In her person action and contemplation fused effortlessly.

As prioress she first directed her energies toward making strict observance desirable and possible for the other sixteen choir nuns and six lay sisters. To this end she gradually reduced the number of social calls to the parlor, collected all private possessions the women had stored in their cells, learned how to construct and use communal rooms (e.g., for wardrobe repair), remodeled the entire compound, catalogued a 600-volume library, refurbished musical instruments, and encouraged their mastery for liturgical celebration in the churches. Most important, in conjunction with the house chaplain, Franz

Joseph Schiml, who was also a learned theologian and became a good friend, a new edition and modern German translation of the thirteenth-century Rules and Constitutions, complete with commentaries, was printed. Each religious then knew precisely what was expected of her, whereas previously there had been great confusion.

Moving out from that center, Mother Benedicta not only established branch houses in Germany, but answered the requests of American bishops for a mission that would serve the educational, religious, and health needs of the German immigrants. From the first house in Brooklyn (now the Amityville community) would issue ten other independent Dominican congregations in the United States. And when her term of office was completed, Mother personally founded yet another Dominican congregation in Racine, Wisconsin. When Mother Benedicta took office in Ratisbon in 1845, the nuns' inner world of meaning was disintegrating. She reconstructed and transformed that inner world by forming a new synthesis between contemplative prayer and apostolic involvement.

She was able to move in new directions because of the oral permission the nuns had received in 1803 for their exceptional circumstances. In embracing direct service of the neighbor and in giving it positive value in the life of perfection, Mother Benedicta was moving out of a second-order stance toward the world. Yet her synthesis was not precisely that of the third order either, because Ratisbon perfection had a contemplative foundation: it sought the greatest possible degree of cloister, the faithful recitation of the entire Divine Office, a rigorous asceticism involving retrenchment in sleep and food. This spirituality was bolstered from elements in the general Catholic tradition that viewed life eschatologically, as a temporary condition of fleeting satisfactions whose one true purpose lay in walking the path of salvation. In a key conference delivered in 1847 which set the tone of her goals for renewal, Mother Benedicta spoke in such images: "With our entry into this valley of tears begins our journey out of it. . . . Heaven, the goal toward which we go, earth, where as pilgrims we take rest . . . all these things remind us constantly that we are wanderers in a strange land" (Kohler: 53). Her admonitions to the community were to walk the path with Jesus, neither straying from his steps nor resting along the way. The formation of Mary Backes in Holy Cross Convent in Brooklyn was cast from this mold.

The nuns in New York tried to live like those in Ratisbon, but there were problems. Crawford describes their attempts to keep cloister and the resultant incongruities thus:

There was a grille in the convent, and in the grille, a turn; each Sister had a companion when going to the grille. They did not go into the body of the Church but into some oratory above the sacristy, or adjacent to it, nor did they accompany their pupils to the church until after 1890. But the choir Sisters went to school, which was sometimes across the street or at least the other side of the church and convent. After children's entertainments, the parents came to the Sisters behind the stage. They saw and spoke to agents, etc., and parents of children, without a grille; took over the church choir, and gave rehearsals in a hall or church . . . they never went out to a doctor or dentist except in a closed coach . . . teaching Sisters never attended a lecture or read a newspaper, yet they were supposed to teach history. . . . Hospital and lay Sisters were never cloistered. They nursed in homes and went out questing alms and attending to all shopping, etc., but mingled freely with the choir Sisters, although they ranked below them in Chapel, refectory, and community room. (304)

Responding to the request of the first American prioress, the local bishop changed the status of the congregation to third order in 1896, after the last of the Ratisbon pioneers passed away. At that time, too, the distinctions between choir and lay sisters was dropped.

In 1876, twenty years before New York resolved its problems, three young sisters from Brooklyn volunteered to establish another "foreign mission," this time in San Francisco. The ages of these volunteers is striking: twenty-four, twenty-one, and seventeen. In Brooklyn, as was the European custom, aspirants were admitted after grammar school was completed (at the age of twelve or thirteen); consequently the community had become "a collection of children and young women" (Crawford: 320). Mother Pia Backes, four years professed, was the eldest of the volunteers and the superior of the band. Whereas it is rare in the history of religious orders to find major responsibilities entrusted to those in initial profession, especially when direct supervision is impossible, it was a good choice under these circumstances. Mother Pia was mature for her years, a hard worker, zealous, devout, competent. She had all the qualities necessary for a trustworthy superior, and there were no more seasoned religious available.

It was her responsibility to replicate the religious life of Ratisbon/

Brooklyn in San Francisco—a trust she took seriously. Judging from a letter received from Monsignor Michael May (her director in New York) shortly after her arrival, it would appear that she had immediately written back home for advice on how to achieve this end. In his response he first praised her for accomplishing a most heroic deed—leaving all things for Christ—and he reminded her that God protects and guides his own. She must not waver or look back, for "a good daughter of your Holy Father Saint Dominic has no other homeland but heaven" (OP 1876, Letter). Then he urged her to practice patience in regard "to the points that are very hard for you," assuring her that with good will and tact she should someday have a chapel with the Blessed Sacrament reserved, then a reserved place for the sisters in church, and finally a separate entrance into church.

In the very first decade relationships with the motherhouse in Brooklyn became strained: the necessity of local decision making (especially in financial matters) in San Francisco was interpreted as excessive independence in New York. In 1886 Mother Seraphine confided to her diary that Sister Pia was acting independently; therefore she and two others were given their fare and summoned for an accounting. All seemed to go well at the meeting at which Father May gave them new regulations to follow, she continued, but on their return to San Francisco they wrote to inform her that they had decided to form an independent community. The twenty sisters who had entered in San Francisco wanted it so, as did the local archbishop. "This decision hurt me but nevertheless I acceded to their wishes" (Crawford: 126). Mother Pia was also emotionally wounded, particularly from the loss of confidence, making an entry in her diary that misunderstandings between superiors and subjects are trials harder to bear than death (Backes 1953: December 31, 1887). She was undaunted, however, in the execution of her original trust. She drew on every known resource to make this new congregation religiously strong, apostolically effective.

Clearly Mother Pia wanted Dominican priests to be the chaplains for her community, but her diary shows that their visits were infrequent and their services difficult to obtain—a situation that continually frustrated her. Instead, the Jesuits and Franciscans often said the nuns' daily mass and occasionally gave their retreats. She took heart when they told her that they found her community to be fervent. It was they who suggested that having a grate in the parlor (November 8, 1884) and having two classes of sisters (March 13,

1894) were not in keeping with the times. She made note of their observations but did not address the matter for many years, and then only in dialog with advisors who were Dominican priests.

Mother Pia's apostolic models were the other nineteenth-century women founders, particularly Madame Barat. As early as 1881 she noted how many solid ideas she found in Sophie Barat's biography (June 26), drawing sustenance from her conviction that "the grace of God never fails them that have no other aim but His glory, no other help than God's" (January 20, 1882). The "courage and confidence" motto that Father Varin, SJ, had bequeathed to the religious of the Sacred Heart and Notre Dame de Namur, as well as his admiration for "manly virtues" in women religious became a part of her thinking and writing (see letter, August 21, 1903).

It is worth noting here that in continuity with the bias of scripture, male bishops and theologians projected their gender attributes onto God and concluded that women who were serious about growing in his image and likeness were well advised to develop male attributes. This advice was most often given to vowed religious, as celibacy freed them from the confinements of that psychic space that patriarchy had allotted to their married sisters; a world of private emotions and affections suitable only for the nurturing tasks of the domestic sphere (Ortner 1974; B. Turner 1984). Religious women were urged to take on male definitions of self (i.e., to be rational, reliable, and courageous) in order to be able to exercise offices of trust and responsibility. Mother Pia had such "manly virtues" as a young woman. Given the opportunity for action that was accorded heads of congregations, she proved her ability to operate in the public sphere, to govern firmly, to manage limited resources wisely.

Admiring the strength of international congregations built on Jesuit models, she designed her congregation to be papal also, though no other descendant of Ratisbon did so. Though she was continually disappointed by her unsuccessful attempts to convince other Dominican congregations to join forces with her so that they could achieve more through greater numbers, she constructed creative alternatives.

She traveled through Europe visiting Dominican convents of high repute. While thus engaged she studied their constitutions, observed their lives, and made known to them, their chaplains, and local bishops the needs of the California mission. Once this network was established, she sent sisters from California to some property she obtained in Belgium (Moresnet-Neutre, 1901) to staff a novitiate for German-speaking candidates, most of whom later came to California. The location was moved to Altenhohenau in Bavaria in 1923; it provided a constant supply of missionaries until the Second World War. Mother Pia also made foundations in Mexico (which now has the status of a separate region). These two foreign countries are the only ones linked to the Mission San Jose Dominicans.

The Dominican motto is "to contemplate and to give to others the fruits of contemplation." Mother Pia secured that contemplative foundation by preserving all that was authentically Dominican, preserving as much as possible of the second-order life, requiring the recitation of the entire Divine Office. Her constitutions were recognized by the master general of the first order in 1890. The diploma of affiliation reads in part: "Since you, beloved daughters, living in community in San Francisco, California, have instantly petitioned Us for affiliation with the Third Order of the Holy Patriarch, Saint Dominic, called the Order of Penance, so as to be able to participate in the indulgences and graces of the Order, We willingly grant your desire and pious wish" (OP 1952: 17–18). The Dominican family ties are bonds of grace and merit, not of law. The master general has no juridical authority beyond this power to define family members. If and when he visits the motherhouse of the sisters, it is a mark of sociability.[4]

True to Mother Benedicta's ideals in Ratisbon, Mother Pia tried never to deviate from the Dominican path to salvation or to rest along the way. She looked to the Dominican friars for the correct format for dining. The prayers, processions, refectory design, and perpetual silence[5] were practices common to the order, though not originating from them. What was uniquely Dominican was the "angelic" distribution of bread, the reenactment of a legend immortalizing God's generosity to the community, God's providence, and the power of Dominic's prayer. It bears retelling because it crystallizes and encapsulates the flavor of Dominican prayer.

According to this treasured tale, two brethren had spent all day begging food for their community of 100. Having received just one loaf of bread, they were returning home discouraged when a young man implored them for their single loaf. They gave it away "for the love of God," knowing also that it could never meet the needs of 100 hungry men. Dominic knew all that had happened to them when they arrived home, and assured them that the Lord would feed his servants. After withdrawing to pray, he assembled the community for dinner, though there was no food in sight.

When the brethren were seated our holy father blessed the table, and Brother Henry of Rome began the reading as is the custom during dinner. But St. Dominic joined his hands and began to pray over the table, and lo, as he had promised by the promptings of the Holy Ghost, there suddenly appeared, by God's providence, two very handsome youths in the middle of the refectory, carrying upon their shoulders two clean linen cloths filled with white loaves. Then, starting with the lowest one on the right side and the other on the left, they set a whole loaf of rare beauty before each of the brethren. (Jarrett 1955: 74ff.)

When these angels disappeared the empty casks were found to be filled with wine, so the brothers "ate and drank as much as they pleased that day, and the next day, and again a third day."

Just as the procession physically linked the prayers of chapel with those of the refectory, so did the distribution of bread unite eucharistic thanksgiving at liturgy with the grace of the daily meal. Praise and thanksgiving for God's gracious love and his material gifts were foremost in the Dominican model.

Many Mission San Jose sisters were unaware that the miracle recounted above involved wine, because their customaries referred only to the bread, but their attitude toward alcohol was relaxed. When alcoholic beverages such as wine or beer were donated, they were served in moderation as a treat on the next major feast. Because some sisters came from families who owned breweries, it was commonplace to hear the hissing sound of beer cans being opened in the refectory. Annually, on the feast of St. John the Evangelist (December 27), bottles of wine were blessed by the chaplain and later one glass was served to each sister when the group gathered in the community room to toast "the love of St. John." Legend held that St. John once drank a cup of poisoned wine without being harmed. In medieval times every household brought some of its wine to church to be blessed on that day: some of the blessed wine was then poured into every barrel of wine in the cellars (Weiser 1958: 130). Sisters interviewed did not know the medieval roots of the custom, but this did not hinder their enjoyment of it.[6]

In the refectory the traditions of the order were faithfully observed by the Dominican Sisters of Mission San Jose. They differed from the friars only in adding silent penances at the threshold and in praying an Our Father and Hail Mary before dinner for the release of particular souls in purgatory. Minor customs such as begging food or dropping the veil over one's eyes varied among the branches by sex, by order, by provincial practice, by evolution over time. Mother Pia did add a point of efficiency. According to one sister interviewed, the sisters had washed dishes at the sink until one day in 1919 when Mother Pia said she saw dishpans at the tables in Europe and thought that method to be superior. Dishpans were then introduced.

Contemporary Responses to the Tradition

When inquiring into the origins of the refectory rituals, question 15 of the interview guide ("Did your founder initiate these practices?") caused some confusion in that the Dominican Sisters distinguish between the founder of the congregation and the founder of the order. Mother Pia Backes held the first position; St. Dominic the second. The spirituality was derived from the order.

All of the pre-1925 entrance group held the above distinction and knew or hazarded a guess that St. Dominic selected his penances and his refectory plan from models already in use.

Three of the sisters who entered in the 1960s thought of St. Dominic as the only founder, attributing a minor technical role to Mother Pia. One of those said she did not "relate well" to the figure of Mother Pia; another that Mother Pia organized the group but was not a "founder" in the way that word is ordinarily used. Two of the ten in this set had no idea of the origins of the special refectory behaviors.

When asked, "In actual practice was the focus of your attention during a meal on your penance, your food, your neighbor or the reading?," seven out of ten sisters who entered before 1925 said it was always on the reading. Another said it was on the reading unless she was sitting at "little table" (which was an option only in Advent and Lent); another said it was split between the reading and food; the last explained that she always was hard of hearing, so her attention was on the food.

Of the sisters who entered in the 1960s some were focused on the reading. Three named "reading" alone as a category and three more said they were attentive to the reading unless they were at the "little table." Two said they noticed the food more than the reading; one noticed only the food; one noticed only the people around her.

Those who entered before 1925 remembered Mother Pia in her final years. In those days, they said, she rarely came to the refectory. Her health was poor; an infirmarian was in constant attendance and usually served her meals in her private quarters.

Those who had some interaction with her described her as stern and kind. She praised their achievements (high test scores on state examinations, a piano recital), sympathized with them if they were ill or a family member was suffering, but corrected them sharply if there was an observed failure in obedience to the Rule.

Both Julie Billiart and Mary Backes were prayerful, practical, and dedicated apostolic women who fashioned their congregations from highly successful existing models. Both found friends of high repute in the Jesuit or Dominican orders who were willing to guide them in the formation of their communities.

Notre Dame's Rule was not Jesuit in every aspect, but its food rituals were in that spirit. Though talking was allowed on days of celebration, most meals were taken in silence and were accompanied by table reading designed to put one's mind on God; many of the meals were taken in physically uncomfortable positions; oral self-accusation was a feature of every silent meal (except for breakfast).

The Dominican women followed a precise ritual continuous in the order for seven hundred years. It allowed no self-accusation in the refectory and rarely used physically uncomfortable positions. It was oriented toward prayerful reflection on the oral reading.

In the 1960s sisters in both congregations had difficulty concentrating aurally. Among the Dominicans three could do so consistently, three more could do so if they were physically comfortable, but the remaining four were more attentive to the food or the neighbor. In Notre Dame only one person was consistently attentive to the reading, three more could do so if they were comfortable, one thought only of penance, and the remaining five were consumed by fear. Posture, gesture, and position in the room communicated more powerfully than the spoken word.

Food Rituals and Gender

The food rituals of religious life were based on a desert theology which, in itself, was not gender specific. The variety of body disciplines and refectory designs that grew out of that theology were not intended exclusively for men, for example, but for communities of either sex.

Interviews with the elder cohort of Dominican women demonstrated an unblemished satisfaction with their refectory design and food ritual as well as a glowing pride in the role of St. Dominic in selecting them. Although they did not see themselves as the proper guardians of that tradition in the sense of shaping it, all were guardians of the tradition to the degree that they lived it. The fact that men initiated changes was not interpreted as oppressive. For example, when I was trying to establish a historical order to events, I asked one sister when her congregation had changed the language of prayer from Latin to English. She answered with a smile, "When the Fathers did." Intrigued by that response, I repeated the question to others and received essentially the same answer. Only their fidelity to a common spirituality was worth remembering. The year was irrelevant. The Dominican family was unquestionably patriarchal, but these women opted for that pattern. The younger cohort of sisters responded differently, answering the questions on change in terms of their progress in formation, e.g., "That happened when I was a junior professed." In addition, many of the younger women expressed dissatisfaction with varied aspects of contemporary patriarchy, but they, too, reverenced St. Dominic and the common spirituality shared by men and women in the order.

Two potential challenges to interpretations of gender unity appear in Bynum's richly documented study of medieval feast and fast (1987), where she argues that the religious significance of food was gender specific. On the symbolic level, she reports, women saw themselves as food (a woman's body is the first food for all human life), therefore they related to the nurturing dimensions of eucharistic piety in a way that men did not. However true that may be of private prayer, what was ritualized in convent culture was a shared set of meanings. The eucharistic piety of the era made its way into the Dominican refectory not through women, but through the reenactment of the angelic feeding miracle of St. Dominic and his companions. This story had an all-male cast, but the lessons on Divine Providence were applicable to and treasured by members of both sexes.

Another challenge worth noting arises from Bynum's case study of two sainted friends, Francis and Clare of Assisi (96–102). Having demonstrated the importance of food symbolism in acts of self-renunciation in the lives of medieval women, she argues that Clare's emphasis on fast and abstinence was a matter of gender preference. Bynum buttresses her case by contrasting Clare with Francis, who downplayed that formal pattern of food use in his own spiritual search. Francis' emphasis was on the renunciation of wealth, of all forms of security and stability. As a wandering preacher he chose to be completely vulnerable to circumstances, indifferent to want or plenty, praising God and trusting in God for all things. Thus, food was not the central symbol of his renunciation, as it was for Clare.

I maintain, however, that there is no evidence to support a claim for a gender preference here. The choice that Clare made to be a vowed religious meant cloister and stability. Therefore, like a monk, the means at her disposal for expressing renunciation were few in number. Restraining the appetites by limiting the intake of food was at the heart of the inherited tradition. Clare had no reason to change that. Other women and men who were attracted to imitating Francis more directly became members of the Franciscan lay movement, thus avoiding (temporarily) any papal restrictions on their charismatic activities. As pilgrim peoples they had no guaranteed access to food supplies, therefore they could not observe monastic forms of fast and abstinence. Thus their food asceticism shifted from measured restraint to "holy indifference"; they were grateful for any food whenever they were able to eat.

Those who wished to be perfect in their imitation of Christ chose various means to do so. Over the centuries both women and men had been solitaries; both had been cloistered; both had lived the common life. In the thirteenth century both entered the charismatic lay movements attached to the Dominican and Franciscan orders. For theological reasons all of the above practiced some form of food asceticism. Those forms differed, but gender identification was not the reason for the difference in convent cultures.

Whereas Dominican women were fully aware that men had shaped their common food rituals and were accorded leadership roles in the ongoing reinterpretation of their common spirituality, the opposite was true of Notre Dame.

Sisters of Notre Dame de Namur knew that Julie Billiart held Jesuits in high regard and that she wanted her sisters to imitate Jesuit obedience, discipline, and zeal. Yet the women interviewed were unaware that Jesuit food rituals were the models for their own, and that their common spirit was forged through the faithful practice of refectory customs. As the sisters had no formal link to the Society of Jesus, they thought they were independent of it. Consequently, when the younger cohorts felt completely alienated from the spirituality embedded in these forms, the possibility of a gender bias in the original design did not present itself as a consideration.

In my opinion the constant use of the floor, the gestures of humility, the oral confessions of unworthiness were most appropriate as correctives to male pride, especially for sixteenth-century Spanish men. Here I agree with Bynum: men who seek sanctity (in a tradition where pride is sinful) need to use symbols to renounce their cultural dominance (295). When women use the same set of symbols, however, rather than apply a corrective to a sinful tendency, they merely reaffirm the reality of the lowly status to which society and the church have already assigned them.

From this perspective constant exercises in humility were always a superfluous part of the training of religious women, but were especially distasteful to post–World War II American women, whose achievements in education and in the workforce had caused old definitions of a woman's place to become offensive. Dominican women were allowed to choose their penances and to determine their frequency. Prostration and begging faded into disuse among them in the twentieth century. Sisters of Notre Dame had no such option, therefore their members became increasingly alienated from their ritual forms. Candidates for Notre Dame in the 1960s unconsciously carried new definitions of self at variance with those embedded in the mind of the church, but knowing very little about the history of the asceticism they were embracing, and next to nothing about the origins or symbolic structure of their own food rituals, they were unable to grasp the reasons for their discontent.

PART THREE

THE CULTURAL DYNAMICS

6

TENSIONS AND VALUATIONS

The first generation of professional anthropologists (Durkheim, Mauss, Malinowski) demonstrated that the analysis of food rituals was tied to questions of ideology, morality, reciprocity, and social relations. In continuity with that tradition contemporary scholars have established that the common meal is in fact a symbolic language (Levi-Strauss 1966; Douglas 1970, 1972, 1973; Ortner 1977). Decoding that language opens wide the doors to understanding the basic orientations of a society, especially its subconscious and frequently inarticulate assumptions. A common meal is not only a symbolic language, it is also a cultural performance. The rituals of eating require the observance of formal roles and behaviors that shape the participants' experience in such a way that they appropriate the cultural orientations as their own (Geertz 1973, Ortner 1977).

The cultural orientations of the Dominican Sisters of Mission San Jose and the Sisters of Notre Dame de Namur are made visible in their rituals. Those orientations are communicated to the members in the gestures, words, and actions demanded by their roles. The ascetic tradition and the rituals of convent dining teach (1) an ambivalent attitude toward food and body, as both gifts of creation and sources of temptation, a tension between grace and nature; and (2) a positive valuation of an ordered universe, a graced officialdom, a cohesive community.

I begin this analysis by locating the sources of food ambivalence in the Christian tradition and by showing how the rituals manifested that ambivalence. I then explore the tension points of the ritual construct (grace versus nature, the individual versus the collective) and compare the microtechniques of control each congregation employed to enhance and safeguard the sanctity of its members. Finally, I interweave the treatment of the social and the symbolic in order to (a) place the disciplines of table manners and diet in the context of evolving discourses on the body, and (b) account for the inability of the candidates for religious life in the 1960s to acquire convent culture through ritual participation.

Ambivalent attitudes toward food are characteristic of many societies because eating necessarily involves a life/death contradiction — the taking of life to sustain life. Every society, therefore, creates its own mythic justification for such ecological interventions. Roman Catholic religious draw heavily from scripture for their food beliefs. Elucidating and exploring the connections between the Jewish, Christian, and ascetic traditions will help us understand the ritual manifestations of this ambivalence.

In sacred scripture God made two covenants with the human race about dominion over life and the nature of human food, one before sin disordered creation and one after repeated sinfulness was punished by the Flood. The first Genesis passage reads:

God blessed them [man and woman], saying: "Be fertile and multiply; fill the earth and subdue it. Have dominion over the fish of the sea, the birds of the air, and all the living things that move on the earth." God also said: "See, I give you every seed-bearing plant all over the earth and every tree that has seed-bearing fruit on it to be your food; and to all the animals of the land, all the birds of the air, and all the living creatures that crawl on the ground, I give all the green plants for food." And so it happened. (1:28–30)

In the beginning, according to the Hebrew myth of beginnings, God willed that human food should be vegetative; the fruit of every seed-bearing plant and tree. In the covenant with Noah and his kin, however, the nature of human food and the relationship of human beings to the animal kingdom was forever altered. "Dread fear of you shall come upon all the animals of the earth and all the birds of the air, upon all the creatures that move about on the ground and all the fishes of the sea; into your power they are delivered. Every creature that is alive shall be yours to eat; I give them all to you as I did the green plants. Only flesh with its lifeblood still in it you shall not eat" (Gen. 9:2–4). The right to eat meat, though a gift from God, was symbolically a mixed blessing. It was a reminder of God's fidelity, generosity, and forgiveness, but a reminder as well of sin and its consequences—perpetual enmity between the human and animal worlds.

Although it was written that "every creature that is alive shall be yours to eat," there was one restriction. The Creator of life forbade the blood of life to be food. The ritual separation of flesh from blood (carried out in the temple and in the home) changed the status of the animal from subject to object, transferring the right over this life from God's hands to human hands (Douglas 1970, 1972).

Dietary regulations proliferated after the Exodus and the Mosaic covenant: veritable catalogs of pure and impure foods came into being. Each regulation grew out of the national preoccupation with the meaning of covenant. All were interpretive expressions of the call to be a kingdom of priests, holy and separate from all others. Food restrictions reinforced this special status.

Food rituals of the Jewish people at the time of Jesus were permeated with the sense of the goodness of God and his creation; gratitude for his saving plan and for his choice of Israel to be his own. In the blessing of bread and wine at the Sabbath meal, or in the eating of bitter herbs at Seder, food was the medium for remembering and making present the wondrous covenant of salvation.

The pharisees and scribes were justly puzzled by the authoritative nature of Jesus' preaching and teaching, for the mark of a holy man was obedience to the law, but he and his disciples were neither ascetic nor observant of all the dietary regulations, a serious matter when food habits witness to faith. His responses to their questions were cause for scandal and alarm, for his actions were deliberate and he was obviously aware of their implications. When chastised for his disciples' breaking tradition by not washing their hands before a meal, he rebuked the questioners for their focus on formalism and their neglect of the justice tradition, publicly announcing his own teaching: evil designs and actions are the cause of impurity—diet can never make a person unclean (Matt. 15:1–21).

Peter needed his own special vision to understand. He needed to see the walking, crawling, and flying creatures that as a good Jew he would never eat and hear the voice that said, "What God has made clean, you have no right to call profane" (Acts 10:15). He needed to see a Gentile receive the Holy Spirit to realize that the "holy nation" was the human race.

The personal body and the social body are analogous concepts:

the categories in which each is perceived are drawn from the same cultural storehouse, and an exchange of meanings between the two bodies continually reinforces the culturally perceived correctness of those concepts (Douglas 1973: 93). When the apostles understood that the good news of Jesus Christ was to be preached to all nations, there was a concomitant dramatic shift toward inclusiveness, toward open boundaries. The elimination of dietary restrictions was the analogous shift in relation to the personal body.

What was retained from the Jewish inheritance were the prayers of praise and thanksgiving for all God's saving deeds, and now for the life-death-resurrection of Jesus Christ. The blessings of the Sabbath meal became the source of the eucharistic prayer of the new church; the sharing of bread and wine was communion for the faithful gathered in his name. All food was good, St. Paul wrote, "the word of God and the prayer make it holy" (1 Tim. 4:5).

With the movement toward asceticism, the flourishing of the desert spirituality and its consequent communal institutionalization, came a new elite—a new holy nation, so to speak—separate from all others and endangered by contact with outsiders. The cognitive parallel in matters of food to this social reality is fear of pollution from outside the body; therefore the enactment of dietary rules monitoring what entered the body would be logically expected. Such a reversion to a restricted view of the two bodies did enter Christianity through asceticism, and it remains a distinctive mark of religious congregations of men and women to the present time.

People entered the desert to conform their spirit to that of Jesus Christ, to do battle with their demons as he had battled the devil. Jesus' period of intense prayer and fasting was demarcated by a fixed and limited period of time, forty days; theirs became a permanent occupation. Means became ends. At first this was not true; desert masters accepted the call to be urban bishops; the proficient moved among the masses to exorcise and heal. Fed by the Neoplatonism and Stoicism of heretical theologians, like Evagrius, and preserved by the teachings of more orthodox disciples, like Cassian, energies were deflected to the purification of passions, and self-mastery overtook ministry on the road to perfection. When bodily realities define a fallen state and intellectual contemplation defines union with God, the beatitudes of Jesus take second place to the blessedness of perpetual tranquillity. When the unenlightened masses and their carnal realities detract from the pursuit of holiness, rules of enclosure are a logical corollary. When the physicality of the incarnation and resurrection are passing stages to a more perfect incorporeality, the goods of creation lose their luster. Pleasure no longer expands the affections with prayers of praise but constricts the heart with fear of temptation. Wine needs water, for safety's sake.

Church councils condemned the errors of theologies that bred contempt for material creation, but shades of Evagrius fell over the brightest minds, clouding their thinking with subtle dualisms, casting physical satisfaction in the role of tempter of the soul, molding celibacy and fasting into agents of control. Whenever those tensions were present, attitudes toward food were ambivalent.

Such tensions were present in the theology of St. Augustine. His belief in the power of original sin made him see life as a struggle for the good. In this struggle the body and soul of each human being could cooperate or compete for available energy. Since such supplies were limited, the life of the body robbed the soul of power, e.g., in sexual activity, causing energy to flow out to the world and be lost. It was possible, however, for fasting and celibacy to contain the powers and redirect the energy to the soul. Listening to edifying subjects while eating enlightened the mind, nourished the spirit, strengthened the individual in the life of grace. The act of eating became charged with currents of opportunity and danger.

In the twentieth century, Dominican and Jesuit authors have described their ascetical theologies in Augustinian terms. In a passage quoted earlier, William Hinnebusch writes that the purpose of monastic observances is to help the religious "leash his emotions and passions" so that by "taming the flesh" they prepare a person for contemplation. Body and soul are clearly imaged as antithetical forces when he further observes that "the passions entice the soul from the things of the spirit and focus its attention on the things of the senses, the observances detach him from material things" (1965: 133).

The Jesuit Vermeersch, in his commentary on meals, explicitly cites Augustine as his source for saying that the danger of food is the existence of pleasure in the act of eating (1951: 371–74). The rules for dining were orchestrated to avert such a possibility; as such, they were the complement of the rules of chastity. Though aware of the dangers involved, it was Vermeersch's opinion that the meal was a positive event because it offered so many opportunities to practice virtue—charity, patience, holy indifference, and the self-control of good table manners.

A common strand running through the above ascetic theologies was the fear of the body—of any experience that produced physical pleasure. Fine food and drink, therefore, were temptations to be resisted, it was true, but eating was not primarily seen as an occasion of sin but as part of the plan of creation, a necessity of life which presented the spiritual athlete with repeated opportunities to choose the good. Those choices, it was believed, had consequences in the spiritual realm that affected the well-being of the individual and the collective. Both traditions planned their rituals to maximize the operations of grace, but they emphasized different aspects of those operations and their effects.

Dominican asceticism is directed toward the unseen but needy other—the sinner or the suffering soul. Jesuit asceticism is focused inward on the individual practitioner. The effect desired is a visible improvement in that person's practice of the life of virtue.

The distinctive traits of Dominic's conception of grace and its operation (that affected rituals of convent dining) were grounded in thirteenth-century theology. They emphasized a mystical participation in the passion of Christ, the power of prayer and penance, and a lively concern for the souls in purgatory. Recalling the opinion of his contemporary, Alexander of Hales, we read that the "common pain of the universal Church, crying for the sins of dead believers" contributed to the satisfaction for sin (Le Goff: 249). We remember that pain was viewed as potential merit that could be applied to the suffering souls to speed their release. Contemplative nuns founded by Dominic dedicated their lives to this cause. Enclosure was no hindrance to working for the spiritual well-being of the mystical body, when prayer and penance constituted the tools for apostolic action.

When the notion of indulgences was widely accepted, the whole merit system took on mechanistic connotations and appeared to operate like a bank account for the communion of saints. Referring to a passage given earlier (Crawford: 303), the testimony of a contemplative Dominican confirms this interpretation of the workings of grace. She described the deep meaning she found in acts of self-denial (interrupted sleep, long fasts, continual abstinence from meat) in banking terms. She believed she did more good for people this way than she could have done by face-to-face interactions, because acts of self-denial were "beloved treasures—coins where-with one may purchase the faltering souls of those who have fallen, or are falling, into sin." The Dominican Sisters of Mission San Jose believed in the power of prayer and penance and in their ability to specify the beneficiaries of the graces they earned. Meals presented opportunities to earn merit for the souls in purgatory. Each day the reader announced the intention by saying, "Dear Sister Superior and Sisters, seat with you at table . . .

Sunday: The souls of your departed parents . . .

Monday: The soul which has the most to suffer . . .

Tuesday: The soul which has to remain the longest in Purgatory . . .

Wednesday: The soul which is the first to be released . . .

Thursday: The soul which is entirely forgotten . . .

Friday: The soul that has no other help than the common prayer . . .

Saturday: Two souls, the one who has offended God the most, the other who has yet to satisfy Divine Justice and has never had any intercession . . .

and regale it (them) with an Our Father and a Hail Mary" (Mother-house archives). The prayers of Dominican sisters were like coins wherewith one purchased the release of holy souls.

Jesuit ascetic practices (and those of Notre Dame de Namur) bear the imprint of the personal struggle of Ignatius to combat his own vices. Once a sexually promiscuous "swaggering caballero" who was completely given over to the pursuit of pleasure and fame (Olin 1974; Broderick 1956), Ignatius needed and devised a method to root out his propensity toward pride and licentiousness. That method was the assiduous cultivation of virtues opposed to his vices. In imitation of the poor and lowly Christ, who willingly embraced suffering for the sake of the kingdom, he cultivated an interior likeness by consistently choosing humiliations, humility, poverty. The mission remained the goal. External penances served the inner man: private disciplines (e.g., leg chain) focused awareness on the need for ongoing conversion; public ones (e.g., kissing feet) exercised the person in the practice of a particular virtue (e.g., humility).

Sisters defined these acts of self-denial by their objective in the order of grace. Dominicans claimed them first as penance; Sisters of Notre Dame, as acts of humility. These were not mutually exclusive definitions—the primary meaning for one group was the secondary meaning for the other—but both age groups in the two congregations denied they were ascetics. Although a dictionary definition of an ascetic is one who practices self-denial, especially for religious reasons, my attempts to discuss ascetic motivations were rebuffed. Those who entered before 1925 informed me that asceticism aimed only at self-control and was a pagan concept; those who entered after 1960 wanted me to tell them what asceticism had to do with being a religious. They had entered to deepen their relationship with God, to dedicate their lives and their works to the things of God. If either of these was ascetic, they said, they were not aware of it.

To summarize the Christian tradition on matters of food, one can say that it was both a blessing and a temptation. Bread and wine were heavenly food of the sacred meal. The presence of food in the domestic scene was reason for thanksgiving and for remembering the Giver of all good things; one ate freely of plants, fruits, birds, and animals of every variety. The notion of temptation was fostered through ascetic formulations and introduced to the general populace through that tradition. Religious congregations, in particular, held the idea that sensations of pleasure were suspect, that the satisfaction and delight of eating distracted the member from being centered in God alone, and opened the gates to sexual disorders.

Fear of pleasure devalued bodily experience. Fueled by the propositions that original sin had disordered the human appetites and that body and soul were in competition for limited amounts of available energy, monitoring the appetites became a religious preoccupation. Attending to the drives for comfort or satisfaction defined laxity; the fervent religious deprived the senses and used external penances to foster control. Despite varied interpretations of the workings of grace for self, sinner, or suffering soul, spiritual growth was linked to physical control, sense deprivation, and discomfort. Rituals of convent dining bore witness to the mixed tradition described above.

The Prayer: Spiritual Freedom

"The kind and compassionate Lord has left us a memorial of his wondrous deeds," the Dominican chantress sang each day. The meal prayers of both congregations celebrated this theme. They drew on the Hebrew psalms and the prayer of Jesus (the Our Father) to bless, praise, and give thanks to God for his gifts and good works, especially for his kindness to the poor. With the confidence of a people who know they are loved, they petitioned for their needs: for daily bread, for mercy and forgiveness, for deliverance from harm, for the reward of eternal life. Praise and petition reflected the trust and hope of the community standing before a God who loves, a God who saves. The evidence suggests, however, that grace and nature pull in opposite directions. The prayers were expansive, but the bodies were constrained.

The Action: Bodily Control

Sustaining an unbroken interior communion with God, a continual awareness of the divine presence, was an ideal of religious life. Grace, spoken or chanted before and after meals, was prelude and postlude to a prolonged internal hymn. Lifting the mind and heart to God meant that religious perfected the ability to keep an interior focus, and rules for behavior contributed toward an environment that maximized the possibilities for the success of those efforts. Spontaneous actions, unexpected gestures, or sounds had no place in the refectory; even unavoidable noises like coughing or sneezing were highly controlled.[1]

The disciplined use of the eyes was designed to screen out disruptive sense experiences. In the postulate one learned to focus downward, never at another person. One was not to look idly out the windows when one passed them, or turn one's head freely from side to side. One was not to gather unnecessary information from the visual field. In the refectory only the servers and formation directors were exempt from these regulations by reason of their tasks. Formation directors tried discreetly to observe their charges without becoming a source of distraction themselves.

To prevent distraction and aid reflection sisters were expected to sit still, feet on the floor, legs uncrossed, posture erect. They were to avoid any "abruptness of movement" or any "hastiness in taking food" (OP 1910); they were to "rise and sit without noise" (SND 1893). In Notre Dame they were also instructed to keep their hands on the table and their elbows close to their sides. They were not to lean back in their chairs or place their elbows on the table (ibid.). Hands did not gesticulate or touch another person but they could be used to signal the server that another sister needed salt and pepper, bread and butter. In the Dominican refectory when the hands were not in use they were hidden underneath the scapular; in Notre Dame they rested on the edge of the table.

The sense of hearing was harnessed to serve interiority. The voice of the reader drowned out any random sounds, and the subject matter being read—lives of founders, saints, and martyrs, treatises on the pursuit of perfection—was the raw material for prayer, the nourishment for the soul. All of the regulations were designed to direct the attention from the body to the mind, to subdue nature for the sake of grace. The ideal of St. Augustine held constant for fifteen centuries; every Dominican Constitution carries his words: "Listen without noise and contention to that which is read to you according to custom, until you rise from your meal; nor let your mouth only receive food, but let your ears also be fed with the Word of God" (OP 1952: 27). The 1939 letter of the international leader of the Sisters of Notre Dame, Reverend Mother Monica of the Passion, restates that ideal: "During meals, they shall not content themselves with observing the rules of moderation, modesty, and a holy discipline, and with saying devoutly the prayers before and after; but at the same time that the body takes its refection, the soul should also take hers. For this end they shall listen with attention to the spiritual reading made during the repast, and from time to time they shall raise their hearts to God." Ascetic theory held that one had to discipline the body for the sake of the soul, or the body would absorb all the nourishment. Both congregations, therefore, monitored the process and pace of eating.

Sisters had to eat quickly but "decorously, without avidity, and properly" (OP 1910); they were not to take a second bite until they had finished the first (SND 1893); they were not to indicate either a preference or dislike for what was set before them (OP 1910). Being indifferent to food was a sign of perfection, a testimony to the fact that a sister no longer treasured the things of this world. In one's true home the resurrected body needed no material food; it would neither age nor be subject to pain (or pleasure)—all happiness would stem from the inner union with Divinity. A fervent religious lived in anticipation of the world to come and had therefore developed the virtues of indifference and moderation which counteracted the sense of taste and its pull toward the material. Ascetic theology emphasized the necessity of choosing between the goods of this world and the next, promising that those who practiced detachment in matters of food would soon be able to taste the sweetness of heaven (Cormier et al. 1916). Reality was dichotomized into a series of opposites: grace/nature, mind/body, eternity/temporality. The first terms of each pair were redemptive, but constantly competitive with their opposites for the allegiance of the human heart.

The Spatial Design

Studying the arrangement of refectory space and the movement of the people in that space is key to decoding the environmental component of the ritual message. With the help of the floorplans of the Dominican and Notre Dame refectories, I propose to demonstrate that data generated from proxemics[2] and confirmed by oral or written sources will substantiate the claim that the sisters were being molded by their environs to own and celebrate an ordered universe, a graced officialdom, a cohesive community. They were similarly conditioned to view the individual separated from the group as having a lowly rank and dependent status.

My first considerations will delineate the connections between spatial design and an ordered universe.

The Dominican refectory was a fixed space: the tables were set in the room in a horseshoe pattern that was obligatory for every house, and the seating pattern followed precise rules.[3] The prioress general of the congregation, the one whose authority was greatest, sat at the center of the horizontal table beneath the crucifix on the rear wall. The past prioress general sat on her left. Her second in command, the vicaress, would normally have sat on her right, but she was also the director of the junior professed, so that role determined her place in the lower part of the room near the reader, whose mistakes she corrected. Three general councilors filled out the bench at head table. The treasurer general and the subprioress (superior of the house) occupied the places closest to the head table, the first places at the side tables. The remaining senior professed sisters were seated in order of religious age (year of vowed profession). Within

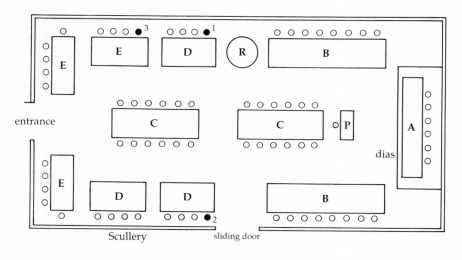

A = Head table: prioress general seated in center
B = Tables for senior professed
C = Tables for junior professed
D = Tables for novices
E = Tables for pustulants

R = Podium for reader
P = Penance table
o = Person
[1]● = Mistress of juniors
[2]● = Mistress of novices
[3]● = Mistress of postulants

Seating at tables B–E reflected one's age in religion.

Fig. 1. Refectory, Motherhouse, Dominican Sisters of Mission San Jose, California, 1963.

that year of profession there was another permanent ranking system in operation based on the order in which applications for entrance into the community had been approved.[4] The order of approval determined the seat assignments for all novices and postulants. The formation directors sat with their formation communities, occupying the first place at those tables. The seating order was the same in chapel, at chapter, and at community recreation. The pattern was broken only in the refectory by the assignment of junior professed as food servers and readers (changed weekly). They knew their internal ordering so well that they could adjust their places in line after a mere glance at the group in the atrium. One's identity was derived from one's place in the group.[5]

The detailed regulations of precedence bespeak the importance of this item to the Dominican community. Order was a primary element in their view of the world, as the commentary on the 1923 *Constitutions* attests:

The correct order of precedence is a matter of great importance in a religious community. In Heaven the celestial choirs are grouped according to rank and order. The Saints too occupy the places assigned to them. The visible Church upon earth regulates minutely the order of her hierarchy, from the humble acolyte to the Vicar of Christ. The same is true in human society, even within the narrow limits of the family circle. Disregard or neglect of this custom would everywhere result in chaotic confusion. (1)

This cosmology resembles that of Thomas Aquinas. In his theology of the universe all created beings are hierarchically ordered to one another and to God according to the degree of perfection (knowledge and love) in the species. (The angels are the highest species and they are ranked by choirs, for example.) The movement of the universe is toward beatitude: the aim of all human activity is the possession of God (Wright 1957).

The cosmological theories of one generation become the eternal truths of the next. In western culture theological speculation on the perfection of creation became a self-perpetuating model for the hierarchical ordering of human societies in accordance with the Divine Will. The structures of religious congregations were rooted in and justified by adherence to such eternal truths.

The Notre Dame novitiate refectory was a semifixed space: the place of the superior was a matter for congregational guidelines, the placement of furniture was not. The superior (or mistress in this case) was the only one to sit at the head of a table: the members rotated around that fixed point, moving one place each day. (See figure 2, p. 118; arrows on diagram indicate the direction.) In the Ipswich novitiate of 1963, in conformity with tradition, the "table partners" (persons sitting on one's right and left) were changed whenever the mistress decided to do so (generally after the entire assembly had moved through one complete rotation). There were only two ranks of people in the room; the superior and the novices. There was no order of precedence within the entrance group as there was in the Dominican refectory.

In the early 1960s the Massachusetts province accepted candidates twice a year; about sixty in August, a half dozen more in February. Since the postulancy lasted six months and the novitiate training extended over a two-year period, there would be four "bands" (entrance groups) in the novitiate at any given time. These groups were given names (e.g., Mother Julia's band, St. Ignatius' band) which corresponded to the length of time the group had been in the novitiate, but there was no internal ranking within the band. In the refectory first-year and second-year novices were intermixed. It was only when a group entered its last sixty days before first profession that its members were separated from the whole and seated in such a way that they performed their own rotation around the mistress for the last time.

The movement pattern, so like the rotation of the planets around the sun, is consistent with an Ignatian cosmology. In his 1553 Letter on Obedience (SND 1947) Ignatius reflected on the topic of perfection in creation and one of the places where he saw such perfection was in the peaceful movement of the planets; others were in the harmony among angels and in the beneficial effects of good laws and well-ordered governments on human communities. Perfection, he decided, depended on (1) distinction in rank and (2) union of wills (in intelligent life). The structure of the Society of Jesus was governed by those insights. All relationships were hierarchically ordered toward the accomplishment of God's will. Obedience therefore is the virtue on which the edifice rests. Accordingly, in this same letter, Jesuits were exhorted to develop that virtue by submitting their judgment to that of the superior and "without any discussion approving and praising in our own minds whatsoever the Superior commands" in all things but sin (par. 18).

Julie Billiart espoused an Ignatian theology of obedience. Sisters of Notre Dame were urged to cultivate the virtue of indifference, an aspect of obedience whereby the individual accepts whatever authority ordains (SND 1934b: 3), a virtue that served well in apostolic communities whose members could be assigned anywhere and moved at any time for the good of the whole congregation. Julie Billiart taught that:

The surest means of arriving speedily at the perfection of obedience is to work at becoming indifferent, that is, to desire nothing and to fear nothing. Holy indifference presupposes much humility, great abnegation of self, habitual mortification of the senses, and, above all, a great detachment from one's own judgement and one's personal views. From the moment that a Sister of Notre Dame has bound herself to God by her religious consecration, she must accept with indifference whatever obedience demands of her. (61)

Proxemic analysis alerts one to see cultural values in spatial arrangements. In the architecture of the Massachusetts provincial house (erected in 1962) the Jesuit–Notre Dame theology is cemented in place. Distinction in rank had assumed such importance that the postulants, novices, and professed lived in separate wings and ate in separate refectories served from a common kitchen. The formation program stressed prompt and cheerful obedience; opportunities to practice holy indifference were a part of that training. In the refectory, chapel, and dormitory areas, postulants and novices were reassigned places intermittently and unexpectedly. These relatively insignificant moves were a symbol of accepting the dispositions of authority in one's regard. Both the patterned movement and its disruption were action signs emanating from and reinforcing theological assumptions: perfection lies in the subordination of relations and in union of wills.

The power structure exalted the role of superiors because it was they who mediated God's will to the members and guided the peaceful progression of the community toward beatitude. It was they who received the grace of office upon election or appointment, participating to some degree in the promises made to Peter (Matt. 16:18) that the Spirit would guide the church until the end of time. Like Peter, they could prove their love for God in their exercise of responsibility for others, "feeding the sheep" spiritually and materially.

The environmental testimony to their special status is their fixed place in the center of their respective power structures. Their special status was reinforced by the tokens of respect accorded them in movement patterns and in symbolic interactions.

In the Dominican refectory the highest-ranking person sat at the center of head table, surrounded by assistants and past officers, and at the motherhouse that table was raised on a platform. The prioress general walked at the end of the processional line, the place of honor, and the movement called attention to her preeminence when the entire group stopped at the refectory door while she passed down the length of the line to sign by bell at the entryway that the community might take its refreshment. If the prioress general was not home, the next in charge performed her ritual, but if the prioress arrived late, each seated figure acknowledged her presence by rising when she passed by.

In Notre Dame authority was placed in a single figure who was set apart from the group more radically than in the Dominicans. The superior (or mistress) was the only person who sat at the head of a table; that place was honored, when it was occupied, by the custom that forbade anyone to pass behind her chair. Other signs of respect included the painting of a colored dot on the bottom of a set of dishes in good condition that were thus reserved for her. The superior was the only person for whom the servers poured the coffee and tea; everyone waited for her to take her portion of food before serving themselves; she was the only person exempt from performing the premeal penances. When she did enter the room, the assembly was facing the doorway: they turned to their places when she arrived at hers.

Formation directors had a dual status. They were carefully selected for their posts and were highly regarded personally. In the eyes of those who appointed them they were judged to be virtuous religious who lived the ideals of the congregation. Their place in the refectory (also their place in procession and in chapel) indicates a considerable loss of rank, however.

Why did the vicaress, for instance, the second in command to the prioress general, sit in the lower half of the room? This question becomes graphic in the diagram of the 1963 refectory (see figure 1). The explanation given was that she was also the mistress of juniors and in that position was required to correct the readers (who were junior professed) for mispronunciations. In interview, however, the vicaress reported that she wrote out the corrections during the meal and gave them to the reader at its conclusion, rather than disturb the entire community by interrupting the reading. If there was no practical reason for sitting in the lower half of the room, then she logically should have sat at head table. The other directors also lost the places accorded them by virtue of age in religion. (Neither of them made corrections during a meal either.) After the newcomers mastered the postures and manners, there was little reason for physical proximity. The symbolic loss of status makes perfect sense, though, when interpreted in terms of the nature/culture dialectic.

Sherry Ortner, in her provocative essay "Is Female to Male as Nature Is to Culture?" (1974) examines the nearly universal phenomenon of female subordination. One of the three hypotheses she offers as explanation suggests that a woman's body and its functions place her in social roles that deal with low-level cultural transformations, locating her closer to nature than the male. Proximity to nature, e.g., socialization of children, is universally devalued when compared with occupations that deal with cultural processes, i.e., the generation and sustenance of "systems of meaningful forms (symbols, artifacts, etc.) by means of which humanity transcends the givens of natural existence" or exerts control over nature (72). In the convent, women held a variety of positions on the continuum running from culture to nature, work that secular society allocated to either men or women. Those whose assignments involved dealing with high-level cultural transformations (spiritual leadership, governance) sat at the head table. They were accorded the same respect given to men in the larger society. Formation directors did "women's work," however. They dealt with the children of this nonreproductive world, those who had not yet completed their transformation from secular to sacred modes of being. Consequently, formation directors suffered defilement from their charges, and this is the reason for their loss of status and rank within the larger community.

Such an interpretation sheds light on the formation personnel's experience (common to both congregations) that they had little influence on the council's decision making when the candidates were evaluated, despite the fact that they were the only professed sisters who knew them intimately by reason of sharing life with them and/or receiving their confidences in spiritual interview. It was as though their ability to make judgments, no matter how highly esteemed before they were appointed to this post, was inexplicably devalued. My research in this unisex society substantiates Ortner's hypothesis that those who deal with low-level cultural transformations are devalued by reason of their social role, and her hypothesis clarifies the mixed rank and status accorded to formation personnel.

Sociofugal spaces augment human distancing. The Dominican refectory was sociofugal by intention—designed to promote individual solitude when eating. Prizing contemplation, Dominicans believe that when each individual is interiorly united with God the whole community is blessed. The placement of tables along the walls, the seating of people on one side of those tables, the rules of silence, the disciplined use of the eyes were all ordered toward a prayerful environment. Spontaneous actions and individual innovations could endanger the larger unit but the formal behaviors and bodily disciplines described earlier reduced the likelihood of the group's being so undermined.

The center space allowed for communal activities, processions, and prayers to frame the meal and to integrate the individual into the group. The common rhythm of the procession, the common rhythm of the chant kinesthetically and aurally catalyzed the bonding between the individual and the collective. The assembly was one body with many parts.

The Dominican refectory is a clearcut example of an environmental design supporting the intended use of the space. Notre Dame is a complex contrasting case: the spatial design and the intention were often at cross-purposes.

The floorplan of Notre Dame's refectory suggests a sociopetal purpose, i.e., an environment ordered to human communication: tables and chairs fill the room and people are positioned on both sides of every table. The written guidelines and the use of the space indicate, however, that solitude was preferred to human interaction at meals. But because the Rule required conversation at table at least on Sunday, and it could be allowed at other times at the discretion of the superior, the tables, chairs, and people had to be arranged so that either option could be exercised at any gathering. Since the seating arrangement did not promote solitude, the sisters had to exercise greater control to assure it, especially in the use of the eyes.

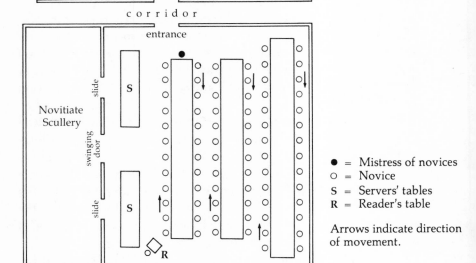

Fig. 2. Refectory, Novitiate wing, Sisters of Notre Dame de Namur provincialate, Ipswich, Massachusetts, 1963.

When conversation was permitted, it too was controlled so that the spoken word would serve the well-being of the whole, not the gratification of the individual. "Recreation" (the term for conversation) at table was intended to be relaxing, but it had also to be "edifying" (morally elevating). While one might expect human conversation to promote intimacy, Notre Dame guarded against it. In a communication from Namur discussing revisions in the rules, the American provincials were reminded of the purposes of speech:

Although joy is recommended to them during recreation, they shall not give themselves up to idle conversation, or to a dissipation that would injure their fervor. They shall refrain as much as possible from speaking of their relations, their advantages, of news—in short, of all that savors of the world. They shall avoid with the greatest care anything in their conversation that might wound charity. They shall converse on good and useful subjects, on topics of holy mirth, and as much as prudence will permit on those that are spiritual and edifying. (1939, art. 84)

The controls on conversation did not dampen the enjoyment of recreation—even subdued laughter was an acceptable part of religious intercourse—but they did maintain formality and human distancing while limiting spontaneity and intimacy.

Members of the 1960–64 entrance groups confirmed that the above recommendations were still enforced (more rigorously in Massachusetts than in California). Sisters recalled that they could mention their families only in passing; that they were to avoid saying anything about themselves that would "lift you above the others"; that they were never to offend against charity or repeat gossip heard in the parlor; never to speak about anything personal, either physical or emotional; not to refer to either spiritual difficulties or spiritual insights. The penances and confession of faults were not to be discussed; nothing "worldly," e.g., former boyfriends or current fashions, was to be mentioned; former members were not recalled to mind; no observation on what another person ate or did not eat was to be made; negative comments were to be avoided.

To whom one spoke was also regulated. The mistress talked to the sisters on her immediate right and left. The rest of the head table broke into groups of four counting down from that set; all other tables also spoke in sets of four.

In this period of relative relaxation physical disciplines had to be maintained: legs could not be crossed, backs could not rest against the chairs, touch was not permitted, gesticulation was held to a minimum, voices were subdued, no one could freely rise from table until the meal had ended. Despite the close face-to-face seating arrangement of Notre Dame refectories and the existence of regularly scheduled table recreations, the overall design was sociofugal. The multitude of conversational rules and a negative touch code were powerful agents of control, safeguarding social distance even in physically close conditions.

Solitude and solidarity were secured by repressing individualism—externally and internally. The spiritual health of the group depended on the humility and charity of the members, on the willingness of each to actually prefer the good of the other to her own.

The Postural Design

Self-effacement was the path to spiritual exaltation. The second chapter of Philippians exhorts the Christian community to inculcate these virtues by imitating Christ:

If our life in Christ means anything to you, if love can persuade at all, or the Spirit that we have in common, or any tenderness and sympathy, then be united in your convictions and united in your love, with a common purpose and a common mind. That is the one thing that would make me completely happy. There must be no competition among you, no conceit; but everybody is to be self-effacing. Always consider the other person to be better than yourself, so that nobody thinks of his own interests first but everybody thinks of other people's interests instead. In your minds you must be the same as Christ Jesus:

> His state was divine,
> yet he did not cling
> to his equality with God
> but emptied himself
> to assume the condition of a slave,
> and became as men are;
> and being as all men are,
> he was humbler yet,
> even to accepting death,
> death on a cross.
> But God raised him high
> and gave him the name
> which is above all other names. (1–9)

As a religion of humility, lowliness is esteemed. In social structural terms, status elevation is won by the ongoing practice of status reversal (V. Turner 1969).

Religious life institutionalized lowliness. Acts of penance (which implied the commission of fault) and acts of humility (which implied the existence of pride) were constant correctives for and reminders of personal frailty. As the Latin root of "humility" implies, postures of lowliness embody and kinesthetically transmit messages of self-abasement. Religious congregations collected and conserved an entire repertoire of such symbols, many of which graced the common meal; more so in Notre Dame than in the Dominicans.

Dominican friars exhibit a decided reluctance to legislate details, but in the seventeenth century they moved to protect the contemplative focus at meals from being transmuted into a penitential one. As mentioned earlier in this study, the 1650 General Chapter ruled that only silent penances could be performed and that these should be few in number, occurring on the eve of a great feast or after the commission of a grave fault; otherwise the common meal would be a scene of confusion inconducive to prayer (OP 1910: 11). This legislation was binding on all congregations within the order, and presumably was the reason why most of the postures of lowliness enacted by the Dominican Sisters of Mission San Jose were used before or after the actual meal, not during it.

The variety, frequency, and duration of penances were extracted from the interviews held with those who entered before 1925. If a sister mentioned her reaction to these practices, that is also noted.

One had to kneel at the doorway before dinner began if one had offended against poverty, especially by breaking or ruining common property, or if one had broken any of a variety of other rules. My inquiries into frequency were always rebuffed as impossible to answer because the penance corresponded to a fault. Frequency depended solely on one's faults. The impression my Dominican respondents gave me was that they considered kneeling a worthwhile and rational custom. It made one think twice; it jarred one into forming new habits. Those first experiences were vividly registered in their minds. Two remembered having to hold their pillows because they had overslept. One had to bring the blackboard on which she had written the wrong versicle for the recitation of Office. Another displayed the book she had left outdoors in the rain. Each of these personal faults had communal consequences and therefore needed a public apology. Those who overslept disrupted the assembly by arriving late; the wrong versicle brought confusion into prayer; a ruined book depleted community resources.

Four of the ten Dominican sisters remembered people prostrating at the doorway and that they had stepped over them (three of these saw this only in Europe), but that practice stopped soon after they entered, they said, not by legislation but because sisters did not choose to do it.

Four sisters also remembered begging soup at the beginning of a meal (kneeling). Three of those four expressed discomfort in so doing because "people looked at you." Begging soup meant that one had to approach many sisters for a small portion from their serving; the interaction was experienced as humiliating. This penance, like prostration, faded away from disuse.

Sitting at the penance table was the only custom that required these sisters to assume a physical position that was lower than the others for the duration of a meal. It was considered the most serious penance, assigned for grave faults, chosen by these respondents once a year—during Lent or retreat. Again, being the object of attention of so many people by being in the middle of an otherwise empty center space, positioned opposite the governing members of the community, was experienced as humiliating. None of these elder sisters mentioned any physical pain from being in a cramped position, only the pain of self-consciousness. Two said it had no effect on them because head table observed custody of the eyes, and those who sat at the penance table did not have to wash their dishes at the end of the meal. These two managed to enjoy it.

Prostration, the most lowly posture, was a common sight during the concluding prayers in the refectory in the variation known as venia. One held that position for a few seconds only. The number of times one executed the venia was not predetermined but depended on whether or not one had been a penitent at the doorway or in some other way during that meal.

Kissing the feet of some of the sisters during the prayers after meals was most often a free choice, although it could be assigned by the superior. The greatest frequency mentioned for a year was five times; most often it was chosen during Lent or one's retreat. It was suggested as an appropriate action to signify sorrow for having offended someone. Two people disliked it enough to permanently avoid it. One of these made an extra effort not to offend people; the other (reportedly) decided she just lacked the humility for it and preferred to live with her pride rather than hope her participation in kissing the feet would cure her problem.

Meals took no longer than thirty minutes to complete. Most of the optional penances required the use of physically low postures for a few seconds or a few minutes and were performed at irregular intervals. I would estimate that Dominican sisters spent no more than two hours a year in such positions: in Notre Dame it was two hours a fortnight.

Pride and selfishness were always perceived as the greatest threats to holiness in Notre Dame. Julie Billiart ate on her knees and drank ashes in her water in obedience to her director lest her spiritual gifts inflate her ego. As a novice mistress from the 1960s confirmed, self-annihilation (defined by her as death to the self that is selfish, ambitious, proud) was an ideal to be cultivated; self-aggrandizement (calling attention to one's self) a condition to be uprooted. The refectory was always considered to be the proper place for conditioning the learning of the soul, a proper place for strengthening in one's self that image of Christ who "emptied himself to assume the condition of a slave . . . and being as all men are, he was humbler yet" (Phil. 2:7,8).

Notre Dame used some of the same practices as the Dominicans (prostration, kissing feet, begging food) but these are surface similarities. The significant differences are that (a) acts of humility and penance were not options chosen by the individual for her own progress in perfection (as they most often were in the Dominicans) but universal recommendations applicable to everyone in the congregation; (b) postures of humility were obligatory frequently and for extended periods of time; and (c) much of the multivocality inherent in symbolic gesture was reduced to sign by the addition of speech, which named the interior state, the intention, or the fault.

Sisters who entered before 1925 reported that before 1921 (when the constitutions were brought into line with the new code of canon law), such practices were not uniformly binding but were individually designed to foster progress in the spiritual life, adjusted for that purpose by the superior after the monthly interview, which included a manifestation of conscience.[6] These sisters lamented the later developments.

When canon law discouraged religious from manifesting their consciences to lay superiors, Notre Dame's spiritual system was thrown off balance. It had to choose between preserving individual relevance and preserving the submission of will and judgment to authority. If it had chosen the first, penances would be options, and as such, some would have fallen into disuse; the system would be responsive to the members. Notre Dame chose the latter; the entire congregation submitted to the will of the reverend mother. Once the congregational recommendations were written, individual relevance was lost. The new arrangement was not only unresponsive to individual needs or regional preferences, it was difficult to change. What had been a simple decision in a local house between two people became material for a General Chapter.

Superiors had been the spiritual directors of their sisters. Now, because some men and women had abused that position, that role was restricted to those who had studied ascetic and moral theology, courses offered in seminaries. Seminaries were not open to women. The spirituality promoted by Ignatius of Loyola when he was a layman was available only to clerics.

As much as they regretted standardization, the sisters who remembered the Institute before 1921 did not think that regulation from above increased the frequencies of the special practices. The idea that grace could flourish only if nature was constrained was integral to the spirituality of the Institute, so penances had always been frequent. One elderly sister laughingly reported that the only anxiety she felt on entering the refectory on a night when she was supposed to beg food was to find someone seated in a chair! (One could not beg from those seated on the floor.) Even in the early 1960s, when each person knelt for a meal twice a week, easily half of the refectory population could be kneeling simultaneously — especially if recreation had been given on a weekday, thereby reducing the number of meals available for discharging that obligation. The visual theme of a meal in Notre Dame was one of lowliness. The visual impression and the participatory experience taught that the poor and humble of heart were close to God.

Speech pinpointed the purpose of the customs and forced each speaker to claim publicly those purposes as her own intentions (even though there might be inner denial of the same). Twice a week in the 1960s each sister asked another to pray with her. The one who initiated asked for the grace to grow in the spirit of Blessed Mother Julia; three virtues of the foundress were named and they kissed one another's feet. Twice a week each sister whispered her failings against the Rule to the mistress and then kissed the floor. Both of these recitations involved an audience of one. The size of that audience was multiplied by 100 (in Ipswich, 1963) for the biannual act of reparation. Its formula, given earlier, is repeated here because of its significance to the problem at hand: "Sister [name], I thank you for your goodness to me. I ask pardon for the trouble I have caused you and that of the sisters for the bad example I have given. I ask your prayers, Sister [name], and that of the sisters, that I may begin a new life."

On the part of the 1960s novice this was an incomprehensible and humiliating declaration. She didn't know what she was apologizing for, unless it was for being alive, nor did she understand the timing. The eve of her saint's feast or of her own baptism were her new religious birthdays (the day of her natural birth was not celebrated); they marked her incorporation into the communion of saints for all eternity. The act of reparation noted the occasion, but there was no festivity, no congratulations; no candles, cake, or ice cream here.

The puzzle comes together when the customs are viewed from the perspective of the tension between the individual and the collective. The Act was supposed to effect what the title implied. Its formula combined the content of the confession of fault (made to the superior) and the petition for prayer (made to another sister) into one unit, to assure the total group that this sister was recommitting herself to the pursuit of holiness—without which the group could not survive. It was meant to repair whatever damage the individual had inadvertently caused the group, mending the rent in the garment of holiness.

Body Discipline: Multiple Discourses

Candidates for Roman Catholic religious orders, reared as bearers of a local culture in a particular age, confronted a tradition-bound constellation of values when they entered; a constellation that protected and supported the ascetic and charismatic structure of the vowed life. Under the watchful eyes of a novice master/mistress one took on ways of thinking and being consonant with one's future promises (e.g., stability, obedience, celibacy) and consonant with a life of virtue as that was defined by the church and one's congregation in that period (e.g., simplicity, docility, mercy, hospitality, penance). The congregation exercised a kind of power that "reaches into the very grain of individuals, touches their bodies and inserts itself into their actions and attitudes, their discourses, learning processes and everyday lives" (Foucault 1980: 39). For many this formative process was merely a disciplined and sharply focused extension of the Christian life imbibed in the home, school, and church; for others it entailed a deliberate break with a past set of behaviors and attitudes. The point I want to establish is that there are a "plurality of discourses with competing regimens of the body" operating at any given point in time (B. Turner: 176). Ascetic elites of the Roman Catholic tradition and other segments of society have articulated different strategies for the production of "docile" bodies, bodies that do what one wishes in the manner one wishes (Foucault 1977). I want to expand this point before I discuss the disciplines of diet and table manners in the context of these evolving discourses.

In his chapter surveying the production of docile bodies (1977: 135–69) Foucault wrote: "The great religious orders had been masters of discipline: they were the specialists of time, the great technicians of rhythm and regular activities" (150). He recognized that religious elites were responsible for developing the discourse on body in Western culture and were responsible for maximizing its potential as servant of the soul through disciplinary regimens. It was the monastic horarium also that established the basic rhythms of life, the time allotted to prayer and work, to eating and sleeping, and the cycles of repetition for each activity. These timetables, Foucault continues, entered the mainstream through the institutions attached to the monasteries: schools, hospitals, poorhouses, and workshops. As late as the seventeenth century remnants of those disciplines operated in the factories: workers began their day in the manner of monks, by washing their hands, offering up their work to God, and making the sign of the cross.

More than one discourse on body exists in a given era. Military forces have always had a vested interest in docile bodies. They, too, had developed techniques for producing bodies that do what is wished in the manner that is wished, techniques for molding a fighting corps that was strong, agile, and precise; one that obeyed without question. As a result of military training the soldier's physical aptitudes and abilities were intensified; the subordination of the individual through self-controlled mastery was likewise intensified (Foucault 1977, B. Turner).

Religious adapted aspects of that training for themselves and their apostolates. The Benedictines (sixth century), the Brothers of the Common Life (fourteenth century), and the Jesuits (sixteenth century) found it useful to organize themselves or their students into working units of ten, for example, called a "decury," named after a unit of the Roman army. In Jesuit colleges these groups of ten were placed under a "decurion" and assigned to fictitious Roman or Carthaginian camps which competed against each other in mock academic warfare. Competition became a classroom pedagogy, one in which pupils were ranked in terms of their value as intellectual combatants. When fully developed in the eighteenth century, Foucault reports, pupils perceived themselves in terms of their competitive positions, which were constantly changing as a result of each inspection and evaluation, according to age, comportment, and mastery of subject.

At the elementary level it was Jean Baptiste De LaSalle (1651–1719), the founder of the Christian Brothers, who introduced the highly admired and widely imitated simultaneous learning programs that enabled poor children from the streets of France to be taught in groups. As they mastered basic learning skills, they learned to master themselves. Wishing to spare them the physical abuse of a schoolmaster's rod and to spare the schoolmaster the frustration of disorder, he taught the pupils to respond to a signal, a wooden device which "contained in its mechanical brevity both the technique of command and the morality of obedience" (Foucault 1977: 166). In this internal management system the students responded to each sound as though it were both the voice of the teacher and the voice of God, a motivation borrowed from religious life. Quoting from LaSalle's *Conduite des Ecoles Chretiennes*, Foucault records the following description: "At the last stroke of the hour, a pupil will ring the bell, and at the first sound of the bell all the pupils will kneel, with their arms crossed and their eyes lowered. When the prayer has been said, the teacher will strike the signal once to indicate that the pupils should get up, a second time as a sign that they should salute Christ, and a third time as a sign that they should sit down" (150). LaSalle's regimen became the standard for the nation by the early nineteenth century. Primary pupils were trained to obey over 200 commands a day, given by voice, by signal, by bell, by whistle. His goal was the formation of Christians. The means was the education of youth in an orderly environment in which the political anatomy of detail was planted in the body-mind-spirit of the learner.

LaSalle's discourse on body and his attentiveness to detail in the educational arena were paralleled by his devotion to "little things" in the life of perfection. This spirituality, cognizant of the gulf between Creator and creature, depicted a merciful God who blessed the intention behind the most insignificant action, who rewarded the love in the human heart. Because infinite meaning lodged in the infinitesimal, every human action had limitless power.

The founder of the Sisters of Notre Dame, Julie Billiart, was reared in this spiritual milieu and in her own instructions to her sisters left written word that perfection in "little things" was both the means of glorifying God and the means of mortifying the self. "In religion, God does not ask great sacrifices of us every day. He has mercy on our weakness. But He does expect, every day, constant little sacrifices, little nameless acts of self-renunciation continually demanded by our Holy Rule, carefulness in all our duties and the exact observance of the least customs in use in our holy Institute" (SND 1934b: 7). Inner and outer disciplines were interdependent factors, but inner dispositions were her focus: simplicity, charity, abandonment to the will of God. Like the Christian Brothers, Notre Dame's spirituality and educational methods were mutually consistent and mutually reinforcing. Classrooms were ordered spaces in which poor children were trained to respond promptly and without question to the sound of the wooden signal (an instrument that remained in use in Notre Dame's elementary classrooms in the United States through the 1960s).

The disciplines of the military and the monastery found points of application beyond those respective realms, chiefly in the institutions staffed by religious. In these units each strategy had a sacred purpose. With the secularization of the larger society, training for citizenship replaced training for Christianity, and the management of populations was ordered to other ends. When medical science and the social sciences advanced other discourses on body and person, religious life adopted and adapted what was useful, straining to keep all things ordered to a divine plan and purpose.

It is this recognition of multiple discourses on the body that is missing from Elias' treatment of table manners. In his researches "politeness" emerges from a seemingly nameless void during the Middle Ages and is dubbed "courtesy" by those who honored it, the courtiers of a budding aristocracy. As manners and dining habits were tied exclusively to the civilizing process in Elias' view, the entire ascetic discourse was ignored. He does mention the fact that a twelfth-century cleric, Hugh of St. Victor, wrote one of the first books on manners, but his explanation is tied solely to the existence of a priestly-aristocratic influence at court or in the training of princes. Similarly, Elias mentions that the clerics of the Roman Catholic church were the agents of downward diffusion, instructing the lower classes of eighteenth-century France on proper manners, but he maintains that a Christian interpretation was introduced at this point for the first time.

My own research indicates that the fundamental discourse on the body in European culture was religious in origin. Ascetic elites, who embraced a variety of strategies for the control of the appetites, were known to have introduced highly formal behaviors for dining by the fourth century. When the additional discourse on manners was developed as nation-states were being formed, religious elites were predisposed to integrate it into their own ascetic system and to disseminate it to the lower classes for two reasons, both of which stemmed from their belief system: (a) they had always held that restraints on instinctual urges fostered the life of grace; and (b) the threshold of repression was so high for eighteenth-century French aristocrats that the habits of the lower classes revolted them; therefore to avoid having the poor consigned to a subhuman species, it was imperative that they be taught "proper" manners.

The plurality of body discourses generated by the medical and social sciences is of current scholarly interest (see Gallagher and Laqueur 1987; O'Neill 1985; B. Turner). In each of these discourses the body is secularized; its proper treatment is not related to a god concept. Integrating the scientific into the religious without diminishing the hegemony of the sacred has been a challenge to Roman Catholicism. An interesting example of this process in the pre-Vatican era is provided by looking at the shift that occurred in the Western world from adhering to a religious pattern of food renunciation to adopting one of food utilization. Both the congregations studied adopted the utilization pattern, but did so for reasons of faith.

Bryan Turner argues that the nineteenth century was the period in which dietary disciplines became secularized, and that "the idea of diet as a control of the soul in the subordination of desire gradually disappeared" (165–70). This process had begun with the advent of Protestantism, which moved the food asceticism of the monastery into the family unit. With the rise of capitalism and the need for healthy workers the focus moved to physical well-being. One's interior state was a medical condition by the nineteenth century, not a moral one. Calories and proteins were of greater consequence than passions and desires.

In the twentieth century, when the Dominican women of Mission San Jose dropped monastic fast and abstinence, they chose food utilization over renunciation. I argue, however, that in convent cultures this shift did not signify secularization. In the Dominican case it marked an acceptance of third-order apostolic status, not a contemplative/penitential one, though they continued to accord high prestige to their second-order roots. When a congregation's focus is apostolic, more weight is given to efficient action, to energy and stamina. New medical knowledge about food, health, and energy was useful for the mission and welcomed for that reason. Food preparation, presentation, and consumption were still liturgically framed. Heavenly feasts had their earthly counterparts, and even in an ordinary week of "ordinary time" there were observable gradations in food service that brought delight in heavenly things to earth by pleasing the eye and the palate.

In this liturgical order the day of the resurrection (Sunday) was preeminent. Monday, Tuesday, and Thursday constituted a middle category, though there was often a largesse associated with Thursday in memory of the Last Supper. Wednesday, Friday, and Saturday retained touches of simplicity in ordinary seasons, and austerity in penitential ones. The proper presentation of a meal did not require the use of foreign foods or specific items; the scale of delight was borrowed from the local culture. Drawing on my own memory, observation, and conversations with former convent cooks, I would say, for example, that a feast day was veritably announced at breakfast by the presence of a half grapefruit, sectioned, sprinkled with sugar, and topped with a cherry. Stewed prunes, for example, would be out of place on such an occasion. Most fresh fruits like oranges and bananas were appropriate for the middle category. The cooks were kitchen liturgists. Keeping a proper religious spirit by matching the tone of the meals to the church's calendar was their special responsibility.

Because Notre Dame was founded as an apostolic order in the nineteenth century, it never emphasized food renunciation. Healthy workers were needed; therefore "A good appetite is a sign of a good vocation" was a familiar maxim in her schools. To avoid making food into a God substitute, a number of controls were built into the ascetic system. One ate whatever one was served, in posturally uncomfortable positions, as quickly as possible.

One had to eat some portion of every course served at each of the three main meals: postulants and novices also had to eat whatever was available at the 10:00 A.M. and 4:00 P.M. snacks. At the latter occasions sisters remembered how difficult it was for them to swallow such things as dry bread and peanut butter, or how they minded drinking the juice, which consisted of the liquid drained from the canned fruits served the previous evening. One ate them without showing any aversion to them. At dinnertime, although one could take small portions from the common serving dishes, there were many courses to be sampled: soup, meat, or fish, potato, two vegetables, two desserts. One suppressed desire by developing indifference, eating what one liked or disliked without comment or reaction; eating at the appointed hour, whether one was hungry or not. The will of the individual was subordinated to that of the group through diets of consumption as well as through diets of renunciation.

All snacks were taken standing and in silence. At the main meal on any given night it was usual for one-third of the community to be taking its meal in penance; to be "kneeling up" at the table or "kneeling out" in the penance area. The recommendations of 1934 provide written evidence that physical pain was important for spiritual growth and that postural discomfort was a substitute for fasting. Some sisters were dispensed from the fast required for all members of the church at large (confessors could give this dispensation). This disconcerted some superiors who interpreted the seeking of such a permission as a sign of laxity. The recommendations required those who were dispensed to eat breakfast kneeling, and at the end of the meal to extend their arms while they recited five Our Fathers and five Hail Marys.

In Notre Dame's twentieth-century understanding the life of grace still required the repression of the natural, pleasurable, and instinctual, while the apostolic life required robust health and increased food consumption. Vigilance was needed to prevent the body from robbing the spirit of increased energy from this source. Postural discomfort was the check on the body.

With Notre Dame as with the Dominican Sisters, the choice for a pattern of food utilization over renunciation was not a sign of secularization but a decision to use every known means to realize their apostolic potential. The diet changed but the body kept its traditional place in sacred discourse.

7

CRITICAL MASS

Roman Catholic religious communities have traditionally under-stood their purpose as twofold: to foster holiness among the members and to provide some service (through prayer and/or action) to the larger church. Where there was rapid social change and gospel ideals were challenged by new constellations of sinfulness and oppression, congregations tended to emerge to give a contemporary witness to the life and hope of Jesus Christ. Yet once formed, they more easily conserved than created, more readily protected than risked.

Religious women were accustomed to rely on the bishops and the Pope for leadership. It was the role of the pastors to assess the needs of the flock and to then invite communities to respond to those needs by making new foundations at home or in foreign lands. Congregations prided themselves on being able to respond promptly to such invitations. In the 1950s, however, Pope Pius XII asked for something else entirely. He wanted to stop an alarming trend that threatened to undermine the whole. He wanted to stop the exodus from religious life that was beginning to develop in Europe, an alarming fact in any era, more alarming at that time because it was accompanied by a severe drop in the numbers of candidates seeking to enter. Consequently the pope called an international congress of major superiors. He told the four thousand delegates that these developments were due to "communities clinging to antiquated customs, traditions that had long lost relevance and meaning to present-day thinking, and that in convents today a mode of life persisted that—internally and externally—was geared to other centuries" (Meyers 1965: 45). The Sacred Congregation of Religious informed the delegates that they would be pleased to receive requests for modernization of constitutions, rules, customs, and ascetical practices.

Since so many of the problems varied regionally, the Vatican mandated national meetings for major superiors. For the first time the women were encouraged to compare their practices, share their problems and their solutions. In the United States the first meeting took place in the summer of 1952; the same delegates then attended yet another international congress in Rome. The lack of persever-ance of candidates for the religious life was again the papal concern. This time the pope counseled the major superiors to "make sure that nothing in your customs, your manners of life, or your ascetical practices raises a barrier or causes loss of vocation . . . for a good girl with courage" (61). In making appropriate changes, however, decision-making processes encoded in the various constitutions were to be respected. Proposals were to be submitted to regularly scheduled Chapters (most of which met every six years) and moral unanimity rather than simple majority voting was to be sought before such changes were finalized.

Congregations in the United States continued to respond wholeheartedly to the papal request to meet to identify prob-lems and strategize solutions, but in the 1950s American novitiates were overflowing with candidates. In fact many communities embarked on ambitious building projects to house the ever-increasing numbers of postulants. Therefore, the call to eliminate trouble-some customs and ascetical practices did not appear to apply with any urgency. Instead, the American agenda reflected the need to reduce the stress sisters experienced from the conflicting demands on their time. What was problematic to them was finding the time for adequate professional preparation (for classroom teaching, for example) while fulfilling their religious obligations toward fixed periods of mental prayer, vocal prayer, and spiritual reading, as well as attending common meals, recreation periods, and household chores.

Another major area of stress sisters experienced was that of inadequate preparation for their apostolic work. It was common practice for many teaching sisters to earn their bachelor's degrees at summer school, for example, so that they often taught for ten years before they were formally trained for their task. Pope Pius XII wanted this to change. He told the mothers general to set new standards for these times.

In the training of your sisters for the tasks that await them, be broadminded and liberal and admit of no stinginess. Whether it be for teaching, the care of the sick, the study of art or anything else, the sister should be able to say to herself, "My Superior is giving me a training that will put me on an equality with my secular colleagues." Give them also the opportunity and the means to keep their professional knowledge up-to-date. This is important for your Sisters' peace of mind and for their work. (Quoted in Meyers: 57.)

This is a significant turning point in the history of religious life. The measure of excellence here is drawn not from scripture or tradition but from secular standards of professional competence.

In the United States major superiors, mistresses of novices, and directors of education met by region under the aegis of a newly emerging organization, the Sister Formation Conference, to implement an educational training program integrating the spiritual, intellectual, social, and apostolic dimensions of the sisters' lives. In 1954–55 the first series of regional conferences were strategically entitled "The Mind of the Church in the Formation of Sisters." As Sister Bertrande Meyers (who spearheaded the movement) knew then and wrote in her 1965 history, "Once convinced that the principles of Sister Formation originated in the mind of the church, mother superiors had no further question as to their acceptance of the movement" (112). The impetus for change came from the Vatican hierarchy; it commanded the obedience of every head of government. In response to this mind of the church, houses of study (called juniorates) were erected throughout the country, ensuring that no sister would be sent on assignment without a proper three-year, postnovitiate preparation. The Sisters of Notre Dame de Namur were a part of this effort. The Dominican Sisters of Mission San Jose, while attending the meetings of Sister Formation, were less affected by it, as they already had such a juniorate operating on their motherhouse grounds.

The educational reforms were welcomed by the members and effectively relieved one major cause of stress in the lives of American religious, but they did not stave off the coming crisis.

Crisis of Culture

My own research and that of Joan Chittister (et al. 1977) on Benedictine women designates 1960 as the definitive year when convent culture lost its hold on the religious aspirant. However, Meyers states that the novice of the 1950s was already different from her predecessors in manifesting the analytical and critical spirit of her contemporary culture (57), and such questioning of cultural values is itself a sign of their loss of power. Interviews with former novice mistresses and others in leadership roles in the Dominican and Notre Dame communities in the 1950s and 1960s confirm that the questioning spirit might have been present in individuals in the fifties but was not characteristic of groups before 1960. In the Chittister volume Ernestine Johann stresses the 1960 date as an endpoint of an era. The custom books of the 1930s, she wrote, were not only unacceptable in 1960, their formalism and perfectionism were now amusing; the lifestyle based on a mystique of self-abnegation was now unattractive and its archaic qualities were seen as an impediment to apostolic accomplishments (9–27).

The women of the 1960s questioned not only formalism and perfectionism, directors stated, but privatism as well. The new candidate was looking for a shared religious experience; she wanted to talk about faith and share her spiritual journey with her companions. Older religious women did not have those needs. They wanted to develop their relationship with God, not with each other. Prayer was their medium for relational development; prayer was personal and private. One mistress of formation who had been in office for a long period of time and had witnessed this transition reiterated this point, which she thought was often misunderstood. The young people, she said, wanted to "bare their souls." They needed to express how they felt but they mistook that need for freedom. They falsely assumed that their way was superior to that of the past and that they were liberated from confining customs. But what this mistress saw were two groups, the old and the young, equally compelled to be the way they were, that is on opposite ends of the vertical/horizontal, private/public, formal/informal continuums, equally unable to comprehend the other's preferred way of being.

The generation gap behind the convent walls was a mild reflection of the breakdown of cultural consensus beyond them. The historian William McLoughlin describes the alienation of youth of the late 1950s and 1960s as the tension of being torn between feelings of being trapped and of being adrift (1978: 196–216). The educational system programmed students into career choices that were unattractive; parental values and behaviors made no sense; nor were church leaders addressing the issues of the age. Voices of tradition offered no wisdom on personal or global life-and-death questions. They had no convincing guidelines for birth control or population control; no antidote to the poisoning of the environment by hydrogen bombs, agricultural chemicals, or factory fumes; no power to relax the stranglehold of the military-industrial complex on the economy or on the individual; no power to remove sputnik from space or the threat it posed for the future from their minds. The Genesis myth of Judeo-Christian tradition that called for filling the earth and subduing it had mushroomed into a technological nightmare. Nature was subdued: the ghost of the future wore a death mask.

The youth of the late fifties sowed the seed of the counter-culture that flowered in the sixties. The beatnik communities eschewed all legal forms of commitment, all middle-class values (especially the Protestant work ethic), and distanced themselves as much as possible from those whose grey flannel minds matched their grey flannel suits (Brake 1985: 88). Espousing bohemian values of spontaneity, expressivity, and creativity, they wrote poetry of protest, defied conventions of cultivated speech and dress, turned to marijuana as a way out of the monotony of the ordinary, a way into a new form of human bonding. The movement was pantheistic and existentialistic: it proclaimed that heaven is inside you, eternity is now. The call was to celebrate the instinctual and intuitive, explore the possibilities inherent in the body for joy. Dismissed by the establishment as irrational and ineffective, they were, instead, artistically rational subversives who confronted "the legitimacy of the corporate, economic, and political system" (O'Neill: 79).

Beat poetry condemned bureaucracy for the toll it took on the human spirit; technology for its sin against the earth; hard work and success within institutions as forms of collaboration in crimes against the self. It drew on oriental wisdom for the foundations of a new worldview, one that sought harmony between human beings and their environment. Unity with nature replaced mastery over nature as a goal.

Since few teenagers read serious poetry, they did not contact the new ideas from that source. The popular arts of the youth culture were the media for this particular message.

James Dean and Elvis Presley were the idols of the mid-1950s, but they were more than stars of the youth culture; in some sense they were messianic figures of a new age. According to music critics

and biographers, both Dean and Presley communicated a liberation
of the instinctual, emotional, sensate self; a deliverance from the
prison of a parental world hedged in by conformity, formality, and
repression of feeling (Guralnick 1979, Dalton 1983, Hammontree
1985, Roy 1985). In the new age defiance was no longer disorder
but enlightenment. For the youth of the era the husk of a deliberate
disobedience protected a fragile hope for a reconstruction of social
value based on the free expression of an authentic self.

In the classic 1956 film *Rebel without a Cause*, James Dean
portrayed a charming, sensitive youth outraged by his family (people
paralyzed by hypocrisy and emotional repression), and by the ugli-
ness of a morally flawed world (Dalton; Hammontree). Dean's ability to embody the wrath of innocence captivated the adolescent
audience. The James Dean cult that developed centered around the
repeated viewing of his films, the imitation of his body techniques
(the slouch and scornful lip), and his grooming style (the unbuttoned
shirt and unconventional hair). Elvis Presley was one of these fans.
Reportedly, he saw the film a dozen times and could recite whole
pages of the script (Guralnick). The "method" school of acting in
which Dean was trained, which emphasized emotion and instinct,
also influenced Elvis' presentation of self.

The success of Elvis Presley's records was due to a combination
of the attractiveness of his image and the attractiveness of his vocal
style. The expressive range of Presley's voice was unusual for a white
singer, moving from "wailing blues" to "spoken growls." Throaty,
sensual, and seemingly crude, its folk immediacy and appeal resided
in the crudeness. "His vocals directly conveyed a restless tension,"
one critic wrote, "suggesting that the lyrics were strongly felt, but
that the feelings were also restrained—as if the moaning could have
been deeper or the wailing more frenetic. This combination of
tension and spontaneity formed the real appeal of Presley's rock
style" (Belz 1972: 42–43).

Elvis disclaimed any conscious role in molding his sensual,
rebellious image. He saw himself as a simple, unaffected person,
wealthy but generous, still devoted to his mother, God, and country.
In his version even his pelvic thrusts were involuntary reflexes.
Biographers think it likely that his shoulder jerks and spasmodic
twitches were taken into his movement vocabulary from his participation at worship in Holiness congregations where such behavior
testifies to a state of emotional abandon to God (Roy: 147), but it

seems that Elvis was genuinely unaware of the influences that produced his vocal/performance style, and unaware that his artistic
"reaction to the stifling conformity of the time could stand for an
entire generation" (Guralnick: 120).

Bioenergetic theory teaches that pleasure is simply the perception of the rhythmic flow of excitation in the body (Lowen 1975:
221). Moving and dancing to rock music, therefore, created a kines-
thetic "high" by intensifying the perception of rhythm while providing an avenue for its release and regeneration. Rock music and
dance produced a new discourse on body that won the allegiance of
adolescents. The amplified sound and resounding rhythm exercised
the kind of power that Foucault described as that which "reaches
into the very grain of individuals, touches their bodies and inserts
itself into their actions and attitudes, their discourses, learning processes
and everyday lives" (1980: 39), a power the ascetic discourse also
claimed. Beginning with Elvis, rock began to function as a total way
of life for the fans. These youth had found the medium for expressing
their own experience, a music both joyous and disturbing, a music
whose meanings could not be determined (Brake: 188). Capitalistic
entrepreneurs rushed in to sustain the market: radio producers adjusted
their programming to the pace of the music, broadcasting everything
—news, weather, ads—in a format of forced excitement (Belz: 45).

By 1960 there were "jarring disjunctions between norms and
experience, old beliefs and new realities, dying patterns and emerging patterns of behavior" that initiated a period of profound social
and intellectual reorientation in North America (McLoughlin: 10).
The generation gap dividing American homes also divided the American sisters.

While candidates for religious life were not drawn from the
rebellious fringes of society, nonetheless they had imbibed values
from the popular culture that clashed with ascetic ideals. In addition,
post–World War II changes in family and educational systems exac-
erbated the transition from one life-style to another.

Directors of formation learned that the 1960s generation had
grown up relatively unsupervised because both parents worked. As
teenagers they had the freedom to come and go at will, observed few
routines, developed few domestic talents. As postulants they found
the order of the day and the regularity of the life overwhelming,
needing to adjust to such simple patterns as eating a common meal
three times a day. Increasingly candidates came from troubled fami-

lies marked by substance abuse or divorce. One mistress said that much of her time was spent in counseling these young women, helping them deal with their problems and then helping them discern whether their choice of convent life was inspired by grace or by the need to escape from home. There was unanimity among these former mistresses that psychological testing was needed to screen applicants in 1960, but such testing was not included in the entrance process for another decade.[1] Mistresses were adamant in asserting that part of the reason why so many postulants never became professed was that they never had the aptitude for the life. High school graduates in 1960 did not have the maturity that high school graduates had in 1940. They were not ready to make life commitments. But formation directors did not have a vote at the council meetings where admission to novitiate or vows was decided. Their opinion was asked, but some had the experience of being overruled. One said that the laundress and the cook had more influence than she did because the superior was more interested in work habits than she was in religious development.

One informant, who had occupied a variety of leadership roles including that of a mistress of novices, saw that even the Catholic educational system in the 1950s was in direct conflict with the goals of religious formation in the convents. She remembered being a classroom teacher when new methods of learning were introduced in the social sciences. Students worked on group projects and chose their own research topics and modes of evaluation. The behaviors and skills she was helping to nurture there included individual and group responsibility, initiative, critical questioning. Catholic schools also fostered leadership training through student government. Girls were guided in the exercise of authority, rewarded with praise for their responsible handling of projects, helped to develop feelings of self-worth connected with the judicious exercise of power or the successful accomplishment of goals. A few years later this teacher was a novice mistress responsible for passing on the congregation's set of values, which included thinking of oneself and acting as though one were "least, lowest, and last." The sound of the bell and the voice of the superior were to be heard as the voice of God, so the emphasis was on promptness of response, not on initiative or individual judgment. She observed that those who suffered most from these mental gymnastics were those who had been most successful in roles of responsibility prior to entrance. Some of the most earnest were psychologically devastated by their effort to assume this new mindset, despite this mistress's efforts to ease the transition and downplay the archaic elements.

Every culture seeks to define itself to its members, to order relationships between human existence and natural forces, to construct a meaningful picture of reality to which all can adhere. Rituals offer such definitions: they dramatize the basic assumptions of fact and value in a culture (Ortner 1977). They begin with some cultural problem and "then work various operations upon it, arriving at 'solutions'—reorganization and reinterpretation of the elements that produce a newly meaningful whole" (3). In the process the fundamentality of the basic assumptions is reestablished. These solutions are fragile cultural products, however, susceptible to being wounded by unavoidable stresses embedded in human existence; e.g., by experiences that defy explanation (natural disasters, war, illness, the triumph of evil over good), or by changing standards emerging from within the group, or by contact with outsiders whose fundamental assumptions differ from one's own. Ritual gathers together these individual orientations that threaten to divide their owners from the community consensus and attempts to heal that constantly recurring cultural wound by "shaping actors in such a way that they wind up appropriating cultural meaning as personally held orientations" (5). Working from this understanding of the process, it is clear that rituals of convent dining were in their dying phase in the twentieth century. They were unable to reestablish the basic assumption of ascetic fact and value in the consciousness of the members, unable to heal the ever widening cultural wound.

The rituals of convent dining were cultural performances that attempted to reestablish the fundamental facts and values of religious congregations—the ascendance of grace over nature, of mind over body, of the common good over individual interest. Both the congregations studied shared a common definition of the situation (the existence of the dichotomies) and a common goal (domination by the superior pole). They differed in their process—the way in which they reorganized and reinterpreted experience—and they were not equally successful in their efforts. In the Dominican congregation, 100 percent of the pre-1925 entrance population sampled said that the special behaviors of the refectory were a meaningful part of their spiritual life, as compared with 60 percent in Notre Dame; 50

percent of the Dominicans in the 1960–64 group could own the spirituality as compared to 10 percent of Notre Dame. In the course of the century the orientations of the members and the orientations of the congregations became increasingly estranged. If the construction of reality rendered in performance is rejected by the actors, ritual is dead. That was the situation in Notre Dame in the early sixties and was becoming the situation in the Dominicans. The forms were empty of meaning.

According to Ortner's model, the purpose of ritual is to heal cultural wounds. It achieves its end chiefly, but not solely, by reorganizing and reinterpreting reality in such a way that the consciousness of the individual conforms to that of the cultural unit. The social unit is never static, however. For ritual to maintain its transforming power, it must also adjust to the accumulated shifts in consciousness that result from social change. Convent dining rituals allowed no such adjustment. Western society in the twentieth century, however, was in a period of accelerated social change and in a transitional state wherein it was reformulating what was good, noble, and true. The rift grew so wide that eventually ritual was unable to reestablish the fundamentality of its basic ascetic assumptions.

"If anyone wishes to come after me, let him deny himself and take up his cross and follow me" (Mark 8:34). The invitation to be like Christ is founded upon walking in his way. To take up one's cross implies a willingness to suffer as Jesus suffered—to be deserted by friends, to be stripped of possessions, to be condemned to death. In the initial age of persecution disciples of Christ had ample opportunities to follow the Master and thus lay down their lives. With the passing of the age of martyrs, however, the way to perfect discipleship was remapped along an ascetic path.

Spiritual martyrdom, as interpreted by the desert masters, was a life of self-denial, of penance and fasting, of silence and sense deprivation. Perfection was sought not so much in active ministry or works of charity as in a life of unbroken contemplation.

When the solitary journey gave way to the communal form, the likelihood of ever suffering from the contempt of society or from the effects of dispossession were further reduced. Abandonment to the will of God was reinterpreted as an aspect of obedience, but external disciplines such as retrenchment from food, sleep, and sense satisfaction retained a significant place in the system also. Biblical passages that enjoined a union of heart and mind among the disciples and passages that eulogized the lowliness of the humble Jesus assumed a new importance. The ideals that were impossible to effect—to suffer martyrdom, to be worthless in the eyes of others, to be dependent on God alone—were kept alive in ritual form.

The common refectory was a ritual arena. In that arena the physical environment, the reading, the human gestures and interactions were oriented toward ascetic goals. The rituals both demonstrated and reinforced the double bias of that culture which asserted (a) that physical pleasure threatened the soul's delight, and (b) that pride threatened the spiritual life. Fear of the body and fear of the individual ego were endemic to religious life.

The Dominican Sisters, Congregation of the Queen of the Holy Rosary, Mission San Jose, used ritual forms that were aimed at promoting interior union with God. Food restrictions were initially honored as a means for promoting spiritual hunger, but as apostolic labors increased, food regulations were lifted. Interior union was cultivated through sociofugal environmental design, external silence, attentiveness to the reading. Practices of humility were included but not emphasized. The individual was controlled through group incorporation.

The Sisters of Notre Dame de Namur used ritual mainly to counteract the power of pride. Eating in physically uncomfortable postures of lowliness and taking part in obligatory premeal and postmeal practices of humility were the means employed to neutralize the negative powers attached to the body and the individual. Attentiveness to the reading and prayerful union with God were also expected.

Religious congregations were designed to sublimate emotional tensions, not ventilate them. Thus the stresses that formation directors and novices experienced were largely hidden from each other and unknown to the rest of the congregation.

Novice mistresses were conservors and transmitters of the tradition. They upheld the values of the special practices even when they were personally doubtful of them. They trusted in the grace of office and hoped that with good will they could faithfully execute the charge to which they had been appointed, though they experienced stress at the lack of training for their tasks and the absence of collaborative partners. Three of the six who held office between 1960 and 1964 reported doubts about whether customs like kissing feet ever produced any virtue, but they felt that expressing those doubts to novices would be a betrayal of trust. Instead, they tried to cope by inventing ways to make the customs credible. Mistresses did not tell their superiors how they felt, either, because such feelings were irrelevant. In the theology of the era, they said, what was naturally repugnant was spiritually beneficial.

There was no uniformity to the explanations offered novices for the customs they were learning, but this research shows that their degree of stress bore no relationship to the content of the explanations anyway. Candidates for religious life had entered another sensory world, a foreign land where space is structured differently, experienced differently, programmed differently (Hall 1968: 84). Foreign environments produce stress on an out-of-awareness level, but symptoms of stress appear when inhabitants do not adjust to their new surroundings, do not feel at home in them. Novices never felt at home with the refectory practices and could not make sense out of who they had been and who they now were. No matter what the mistress said at instruction, the performance experience was a more powerful teacher of religious identity.

In Notre Dame the postures and gestures employed conveyed an attitude toward the self that was diametrically opposed to the one imbibed at home and in school. Personal orientations that derived from the novices' culture conflicted with religious orientations of the congregation over the value of the self. Dis-ease was present even in the first quarter of the century, but by 1960 candidates were highly stressed. Belonging meant participating but conformity was external. The rules forbade speaking to each other about the penances or their spiritual life, so their illness remained untreated.

No one knows precisely when the rituals died, when the actors rejected the construction of reality rendered in performance, when the forms became empty, because no one inquired at the time. The ascetic inheritance had endured for more than fifteen hundred years; that it could some day fail to win the allegiance of dedicated Christian youth was unthinkable.

Religious life is a response to the call to follow Christ. The understanding of what the call means and how the response should be formulated needed a totally new theological interpretation. That reinterpretation, the guidelines for the adaptation and renewal of religious life, was constructed by the bishops and theologians at the Second Vatican Council. Vatican II ushered in a new age.

EPILOGUE

The catalyst for the renewal of religious life, *The Nun in the World*, was authored by a Belgian cardinal, Leon Joseph Suenens, in 1961 (translated into English in 1962). The sharp decrease in European vocations and the devaluation of religious life (even in the eyes of its traditional supporters) led him to look for explanations in the conflict between convent values and contemporary Western values. He proposed that the unquestioning acceptance of traditional ways was as meaningful as feudalism to the modern mind and that "everything that reminds people of the manners of an earlier age, the artificial etiquette of Courts, certain bourgeois customs and conventions, marks of respect in so far as they are pompous or obsequious—all these belong now to the past" (5). Since refectories were the very centers of learning for all the behaviors he opposed, those who embraced his reforms called the rituals of dining into question.

Cardinal Suenens did not mince words. Convents were the last stronghold of studied manners of the last century, he observed, and nuns the decorative wax flowers. If religious life had a future it would have to embrace what was good in the popular culture; develop an appreciation of personal values—freedom, responsibility, inventiveness, creativity, equality, and above all human solidarity.

Suenens reviewed for his readers the history of women founders in the sixteenth and seventeenth centuries whose apostolic wings were clipped by powerful men unable to envisage holiness outside concrete walls protecting women's "virtue" (virginity). He exhorted them to read this moment in history as the founders would have read it, as opportunity for their original visions to be enfleshed. In most societies women's safety was adequately protected by the law

145

and the police. In addition feminists had forced open the doors to a variety of educational and vocational opportunities that could lead to the betterment of the human condition, and Catholic lay women had pioneered in serving the poor in remote locations in hardship conditions. Could religious do less? Not if it were true that "the only reason for consecrating one's life to God for the salvation of the world is to achieve a greater apostolic radiancy than one could in the world" (65). Why, he asked them, did they not take Pope Pius XII's call to update their customs and learn from secular society more seriously?

This startling publication was not yet "the mind of the church" but the work of one theologian, albeit a high-ranking ecclesiastic. However, many correctly surmised that it foreshadowed the thinking of the upcoming Vatican Council (1962–65). It should be noted, though, that when *The Nun in the World* was published, sisters did not automatically have free access to it. Those in authority considered censorship their responsibility. It was possible for a major superior or provincial to order all local superiors to pull a work from their shelves. (One such incident in the sixties was reported to me.) Barring such interventions the procedure was for local houses to purchase one copy of a new title: the superior perused it and then decided if anyone else would do so. If she found it especially valuable, she might choose it for table reading. In large houses, such as motherhouses or provincialates, new books circulated first among the high-ranking professed; junior professed, by contrast, were often given the classics for their spiritual reading. At the bottom of the information pole stood the novices. Though the future of religious life was the critical question, only rarely were those with the greatest stake in the future invited to study or discuss it before Vatican II published "The Decree on the Renewal of Religious Life" in October of 1965.

The Second Vatican Council, unlike all previous councils, did not convene to deal with heresy. Its agenda was pastoral. Its concerns were with witness, the nature of the church, its mission to evangelize, the ecumenical dimensions of that mission, the vitality and comprehensibility of liturgical life in each culture. Such a global agenda required a close examination of the desired relationship between the church and the world, between salvation history and historical event.

Scripture and all subsequent Christian literature exhibit denotative and connotative confusion in regard to the "world," therefore the members of the council had to disentangle the uses of the word. The major tradition emerging from the Genesis myth and supported by the gospels spoke of creation as the work of God's hands, a work of love, and the motivation for the incarnation/redemption event was that eternal love for the world. Yet another line of thought claimed that the world was in the power of the evil one and Christians should not love the world or conform themselves to the world (1 John 2:15–17; Rom. 12:2). Church tradition often spoke out of the second mode—condemning the condition wherein vanity and malice had transformed human energies intended for the service of God and neighbor into energies at cross-purposes to that divine plan (Butler 1981: 187). Consequently, in the language of the tradition, the "world" was distinguished from the "church" in such a way as to suggest that a person could belong to only one.

When Segundo puzzled over the origins of the pejorative connotation attached to "world," he observed that the prologue to the gospel of St. John actually used the one term to designate three separate realities: (a) creation, (b) humanity, (c) that portion of humanity that rejects the Word. But in the rest of the gospel "those who deny the Word, and only they, are 'the world.' One can say that the whole Gospel of John does nothing else but depict a battle between Jesus and this 'world.' Jesus certainly emerges victorious, but that does not finish off the 'world.' As Jesus himself foresees, the world will continue to operate on those who will carry on his message and attitudes" (1973: 80). In Segundo's analysis the spirit of the world, in its pejorative connotation, is more than personal malice. It is a structure that represses liberty. In its systematized determinism the world values only what comes from itself.

For the world is a system of desires which are sparked and snuffed out within itself, a system of thoughts wherein one listens only to what he already knows, and a social system wherein one loves only what he has always loved already [ibid.]. . . . It is the force of a natural world that has already been neatly systematized; in it hate and love are already fashioned once and for all, knowledge and prestige are handed out readymade, and desire is sated as soon as it is expressed. (81)

The mission of Jesus and of the disciples, as well as the mission of the church in the contemporary world, is to break open this system which suppresses human potential to love more than itself.

The gospel of John is the main source of ambiguity of the term "world," but distinguishing the meanings eliminates the confusion. The human community that is united to the liberating action of Jesus is the "world"; the locus of the liberating action is the "world" that God made and loves; and the evil force is the oppressive "world." The source of liberty from that oppression is the revelation of Jesus Christ. Its origin is outside the natural world but is realized both in historical time and in eschatological time. These two dimensions of time enrich the Christian perception of life and give it direction. For those who have the mind of Christ Jesus, the love of God embraces the love of neighbor and stranger, friend and enemy, and in this love the face of the earth is renewed.

Whenever a religion claims that a god preexists the world, it must grapple with the nature of and relationship between the two dwelling places and the valuation of time. In his chapter on "Eschatology and History," Butler observed that council members at Vatican II were not always aware that they operated out of different valuations, but in fact latent tensions over this issue were likely to erupt at any moment. Those who favored an essentialist view of the church, who claimed that the truths of the faith are unchanging, locked horns with the existentialists who focused on the church as Christ now present to the contemporary suffering and aspiring world. The tension permeates the documents and is never fully resolved, Butler claims, but the existentialists won significant debates. One of these concerned the basic image to be used to describe the reality of the church. Essentialists spoke in behalf of "the mystical body of Christ" which is the glorified body—beyond the reach of historicity. Existentialists backed the motif that was chosen—"the people of God"—which connotes historical reality and evolutionary time. The essentialists were also defeated on the issue of whether or not to include a confession of sinfulness on the part of the church. They opposed such a statement on the grounds that the Creed names the church as "holy"; therefore it is without stain of sin. Instead, the council members voted to confess that the church is and always will be in need of purgation; for sin wreaks havoc on the world and that sin does not stop at the door of the church. Nor does the Roman Catholic church have a monopoly on the grace of God. The "Dogmatic Constitution on the Church" grants that the Spirit of God is operative outside the institutional church and in the lives of people who do not know the gospel of Jesus Christ. If the possibilities for grace are everywhere, then the boundaries of the church as people of God can never be drawn. The church and the world of graced humanity are interpenetrable realities. In the same way there is only one human vocation and one history: salvation history is human history interpreted in the light of revelation. It enables people to comprehend the profundity of their existence and their destiny (Segundo: 95).

In his commentary on the *Decree on the Appropriate Renewal of the Religious Life* (1966: 9–55) Baum observes that the usual interpretation given to the story of the rich young man (Matt. 19:16–22)— invitation to leave the world and enter into a life of perfection—is a false one. Biblical studies attest to the indubitable fact that the state of perfection is the baptismal state and that the counsels and beatitudes are addressed to all the faithful, not a chosen few. At Vatican II the bishops confirmed the universal nature of the call to holiness thus:

The Lord Jesus, the divine Teacher and Model of all perfection, preached holiness of life to each and every one of his disciples, regardless of their situation: "You therefore are to be perfect, even as your heavenly Father is perfect" (Mt 5.48) . . . The followers of Christ . . . are warned by the Apostle to live "as becomes saints" (Eph 5.3), and to put on "as God's chosen ones, holy and beloved, a heart of mercy, kindness, humility, meekness, patience" (Col 3.12), and to possess the fruits of the Spirit unto holiness (cf Gal 5.22; Rom 6.22) . . . Thus it is evident to everyone that all the faithful of Christ of whatever rank or status are called to the fullness of the Christian life and to the perfection of charity. (*Dogmatic Constitution on the Church*, Ch. 5, par. 40, in Abbott [1966])

It was necessary to spell this out again because religious life had come to represent a special state of perfection higher than that of the laity, lower than that of the cleric. Vatican II expressly denied that such a hierarchy of holiness exists (Ch. 6, par. 1). Religious life, they said, does not belong to the hierarchical structure of the church but to its charismatic structure. A vocation is a grace, freely given and freely received, intended to enrich the whole community. Religious are distinguished from the laity only in belonging to a specific structure designed to be a sign of the kingdom of God and having as its express purpose the facilitation of the following of Jesus Christ (Baum: 11).

For centuries convent customs and figures of speech, spiritual literature, spiritual direction, and popular preaching had emphasized differences between religious and laity, instead of similarities. Consequently, when Pope Pius XII urged religious leaders to drop antiquated customs, the major superiors hesitated to do so because religious life appeared to be the sum total of its differences from the surrounding secular culture. Language codes reinforced the distinctions. People outside canonically approved structures were termed "seculars" by the insiders: "seculars" lived "in the world." In this phraseology "world" did not connote the graced humanity of Vatican II thought but an uncommitted Christian life (Baum: 13). Ceremonies of profession emphasized the renunciation of one's past, not the full flowering of baptismal grace. Communities of Jesuit descent often sang this prayer at these ceremonies, "Take, Lord, receive my liberty, my memory, my entire will" and thereafter did not speak of their biological families or preentrance accomplishments; nor did they eat in the presence of laity. It was not a theological doctrine that professed religious were members of a superior caste, holy and separate, but patterns of living that had emerged in the fourth and fifth centuries took on an aura of immutability which constitutions and canon law cemented into a functional reality of caste.

Baptism was the focal point of a reconstructed picture—all people and activities derived their place and purpose from that grace. The common bond of baptism knew no privileged classes or any sacred/profane dichotomies. The common call to holiness and the common responsibility for evangelization fashioned graced links between men and women, religious and lay. Vatican II announced no new dogmas but it gave the universal church a dramatic face-life, revealing a refreshingly updated image to its Catholic sons and daughters, to its Protestant sisters and brothers, an image clearly rooted in the Bible and speaking out of scriptural metaphors rather than in scholastic terms. During the council sessions theological certitude gave way to theological explorations, uniformity to pluriformity; essentialists made room for existentialists, metaphysicians for psychologists and sociologists. As a result of the council, religious enclosures opened their doors, and like their founders before them, men and women became architects of their own future.

The structural principles of the new architectural design were given in the council's document addressed to religious. It required that each congregation adjust its manner of life, prayer, and work to the physical and psychological conditions of the members and to the economic and social circumstances of the surrounding culture (*Decree on the Appropriate Renewal of the Religious Life,* par. 3, in Baum.) In the process of updating their constitutions and customaries religious were also reminded that the inspiration of their founder was to be maintained, but the accounts of discipleship found in the gospels and epistles were to be the primary models for the renewal (par. 2). The biblical images of sharing selected by the bishops and cited by the documents, such as "the company of the believers were of one heart and soul" (Acts 4:32) and "a community gathered together as a true family in the Lord's name enjoys his presence" (Matt. 18:20) called the internal orientation of the dining rituals into question.

Both the Dominican and Notre Dame sisters dropped their silent meals and their penances in the period of experimentation that followed the council. A dining room in a convent today has no fixed features; grace before meals has no fixed form. A key symbol of the past religious culture has been discarded. Such an action has consequences in the present.

In terms of the spirit-body dynamic, the thinking that the body had to be restricted for the sake of the spirit was outmoded and rejected by post-1965 popular American culture. In the United States grace and nature were not seen as competing forces; instead, the body and spirit were considered to be one interdependent unit. Yoga and yogurt, physical fitness and health foods were the new wholistic disciplines. While the intensity of interest in those particular tools has subsided, religious and laity alike image the person as a body-soul unity which needs attention and nourishment, an opinion that meshes with a post-Vatican incarnational theology.

In regard to the individual-collective dynamic the implications are more complicated. In the matter of table reading, for example, sisters in the two age groups interviewed noted its passing with some regret. The older group reported that in their opinion shared reading built community by enriching the imagination, touching points of inspiration, providing common food for thought which could be pursued in other periods of conversation. Some younger sisters mentioned, also, that there are lacunae in their bonding from lack of common knowledge, a dearth of common experiences. Inspiration and orientation are individualized and lack a way to surface in, or be critiqued by, a communal forum. In this period of experimentation the current conversations have been sharply focused around rewriting constitutions. At this juncture members have been immersed in studying their past and reinterpreting it in the light of the present. To a large extent this involvement has replaced shared table reading in keeping alive the knowledge of the original charism and the congregational story. When this period passes, it is unclear what the loss of common exposure to congregational ideals will mean for new members.

The analysis of dining showed that Dominicans valued the fixed place and a finely tuned unison corporate movement. Notre Dame, in contrast, kept moving (obediently) and practiced a studied indifference to place or partner. These patterns reappear in the respective congregations' post-Vatican designs for community and mission. (For the sake of illustrating contrasting choices within one geographic region, I refer only to the California province of Notre Dame for 1986 statistics; likewise the Dominican numbers exclude their German and Mexican regions.)

	OP	SND
Number of members	315	243
Number of local residences	23	115
Average size of local community	13.7	2.1
Number who live "singly"[1]	0	18
Number who live alone	0	30

In light of the above table and with a knowledge of their prayer traditions, it is possible to comment on the effect of dropping the food rituals.

The common meal was the one ritual arena wherein Notre Dame formally stated its identity. In the days when the old ritual harmonized with the worldview of the members, the refectory behaviors were daily reminders of common faith, mutual dependence, unity of purpose, confession of fault, and ongoing conversion of life. Today the local group is responsible for devising its own way of creating that sacred space where members can share their faith journey. The ability to do so is complicated by the rapidity with which sisters move and recombine in small groups and by the fact that their prayer tradition is basically one of private meditation, though participation in liturgical prayer is encouraged (SND 1984b: directive 25). In Notre Dame there are no symbolic forms common to the international congregation or the intermediate units that are capable of nourishing the faith of the members as the food rituals once did in the age of the founders.

The present *Constitutions* (1984) focus on mission. Therefore they encourage inculturation, local policy-making, and individual freedoms and responsibilities. In regard to prayer, for example, one directive states: "Each sister has a responsibility to herself and to the community to establish a habit of prayer which fosters and enriches her life of faith and mission" (directive 23), but there are no structures of accountability for implementing that directive. Those entrusted with governance of the congregation have no systematic way of knowing if the directive is effective or ineffective. This is also true of the prayer forms recommended for the local community: it is accountable to itself. The high level of autonomy accorded the individual and the local house, as well as the absence of structures for accountability in regard to prayer serve to privatize faith and render the sacred center (which is presumed to animate action) mute. As collective control diminishes, so does sacred discourse and its potential to unify experience and order it toward the ultimate dimensions of existence.

In the California unit individualized and privatized experience is most pronounced because of the living patterns. The forty-eight sisters who live apart or alone serve the province well by working on committees, task forces, and assembly groups, but in these contexts they do not necessarily pray together or formally share a common meal. The sisters are currently assessing the effects of these choices. In their "Internal Environment Study" (SND 1986) Sisters of Notre Dame in all age groups in California named their greatest stress as the uncertainty of their commitment to one another (12). They are concerned, too, about their ability to attract new candidates. Current membership lists for the California province show that only eight made first profession between 1970 and 1980; one more did so in 1986.

Though vocations have declined markedly since the late fifties for all religious congregations, comparatively speaking the Dominican community is doing well. Thirty-three of their present members made vows between 1970 and 1980; eighteen more have done so since 1981. The Mission San Jose community is the most ethnically mixed congregation in California and a number of minority candidates continue to choose this congregation, reportedly because of its collective emphasis and clear identity. It has retained such an identity because of its conservative stance: the sisters are intent on preserving what they value from the past while they cautiously modify their practices and processes to meet the needs of the American person in the modern age. Ever respectful of and responsive to the church hierarchy, they have responded to Vatican II's call for *aggiornamento* without radically altering their basic interpretations of governance, ministry, or community.

In regard to governance, for example, in the pre–Vatican II era sisters were told what their work assignment would be for the coming year. Now the missioning process can begin either from the prioress general and her councilors or from the individual, if she wishes to request a move. In either case there is opportunity for dialog. In their last Chapter (1985) they cautiously explored the possibility of greater diversity in their works, naming as points of consideration the need for discerning the impact of diverse ministries on "quality Dominican life" and on their identity (art. 8).[2] There is now a task force on personnel placement that has issued guidelines for such situations as requests to move from a corporate to an individual work. In the spring of 1987 three sisters requested such a move; two asked to return from individual to corporate works.

The Dominicans' commitment to the recitation of the Divine Office requires that the local house consist of no fewer than three sisters.[4] Each house has a superior who is responsible for providing spiritual leadership within her convent and for ordering the day-to-day decisions toward the common good of all. Each house is considered to be a "cloister," but now the local unit defines how strictly or liberally cloister will be observed. Each superior is expected to know where her sisters are, however, so they provide her with that information, as well as request her permission to absent themselves from community for long periods of time, e.g., for family vacations.

The current Dominican constitutions continue to emphasize the importance of unity, common identity, and physical presence to community. Wearing a modified habit and veil, they gather daily for meals and prayer. The common meal is called a sign and instrument of their unity in Christ (art. 11), therefore regular attendance is expected. Twice a day, also, the sisters gather to sing hymns, chant psalms, and briefly speak their personal and global concerns in a framework of intercessory prayer. It is in this area, balancing one's presence to community with one's presence to ministry, that the sisters most commonly experience tension, a general councilor told me.

When I asked this same person if the sexist language of existing prayers was an issue for them or a considerable source of tension, she replied that their liturgy committee promulgated guidelines that urged the use of inclusive language in vocal prayer wherever possible, but scripture was exempted from such adaptation. The reason given for this exemption was that there was an official inclusive language translation of scripture that was known to be in process; therefore, until that was published, in the interests of harmony in the recitation, God would remain "He." In this councilor's opinion, this interim period was intensely painful for some, but the discomfort was not universal. Asked if she could identify the segment of her population for whom it was painful, she responded that the variable was one's exposure to the issue in all its ramifications. Such exposure to this and other issues was an individual matter.

The two congregations studied consign different material to the private sphere of individual interest. For Notre Dame it is prayer. For the Dominicans it is social consciousness.

Each congregation brings a different set of gifts to the universal church, gifts that sprout from self-definitions rooted in the group history and charism. Both of the above congregations remain in the process of renewal, of creating those internal structures and ways of being that are consistent with the past, meaningful and viable for the future. Whether or not they are successful in those attempts will be decided by the present and future candidates for religious life.

It is unlikely that in the near future any United States community will attract the numbers of candidates it once had in the 1950s. This does not necessarily mean that religious life is dying, only that it is adjusting to more normal conditions after an abnormal influx in the postwar period. Such is the opinion of the papal commission that studied the decline in vocations in the United States (Quinn 1986). They reported to the U.S. bishops that the reason for the surge in vocations between 1945 and 1960 was the fact that returning veterans displaced female workers from their public service careers. Some of these women, and others who were about to enter the marketplace, chose religious life as an alternative to the confines of domestic life. Thus the church provided an outlet for the meaningful exercise of personal, intellectual, and managerial skills in this period.

Now, of course, that situation is reversed. Women who wish to improve the quality of life for the disabled, the elderly, the unemployed, or the homeless, for example, can do so through legal, political, or medical careers, or by joining political networks that lobby for environmental protection, human rights, peace, and justice. The consciousness-raising process that accompanied the women's movement has also made religious life a less likely choice, exposing as it did the whole clerical caste system of the Roman ecclesia and its subordination of women.

Yet, as the commission also noted, the United States still has one of the highest numbers of candidates for religious life of any country in the world. Though it contains only 6 percent of the world's Catholic population, it provides 32 percent of the world's novices.

Albert DiIanni, the vicar general of the Marists, has also written on the problem of declining vocations, particularly in progressive communities. He strikes at the heart of the matter, in my opinion, when he maintains that the greatest danger to the future of religious life is the laicization of its content. Unfortunately, the majority of progressive orders, he observes, dropped the symbolic vehicles that carried their myths without replacing them, losing in the process the "sense of sacred time and sacred space and sacred persons consecrated in a special way to something which transcends the world" (1987: 208). In shedding outmoded approaches to the sacred, he maintains, they unwittingly moved toward espousing a nonreligious Christianity. It is the eschatological dimension that is essential, however: good works are not enough. Without sacred symbols "religious life has no face. . . . It is no longer a form of life that throws the life of Christ into literal and dramatic relief in the world. It is a religious life devoid of élan partly because it lacks a distinctive and concrete embodiment" (209). What is needed is the "creation of new 'conditions of prayer,' structures of personal and communal prayer and worship that serve to bring the Gospel to life in the members and to foster the constant conversion and sanctification of their hearts—structures that while directing them outward to the mission, also remind them that the center of religious life is the Incarnation and the Resurrection of the Lord" (210).

Throughout the earth food is a symbol for life, and the sharing of food a sign and pledge of bonding. The common meal is a sacred event which nourishes those who name and shape its potency. The religious women who survive these transitional times will be among those who resist the forces of secularism by seizing and celebrating the graced moments of existence, among those who plait each strand of being into designs of blessing, into messages of hope.

In addition to embodying an eschatological witness, the congregations in the United States must respond to contemporary theological and cultural understandings of the virtuous and good. Creation and liberation theologies call for passion and engagement on the personal and political levels for the sake of the people and the planet. Thus, congregations who once marked progress in the spiritual life by the presence of tranquility and the control of the senses must now form their candidates in well-directed patterns of release and regeneration of energy. They must harness the individual's talents for the service of others while challenging her to ever greater creativity in the exercise thereof. The mission of the group must be so clearly focused, that even with diversity of ministries, the sister will have reason to believe that more can be accomplished within the congregation than she would be likely to achieve alone. It would mean, too, that while exercising responsible stewardship over her God-given talents, the individual would continue to author her life by having voice and vote in the governance of her community and by having the right to express dissent when her conscience so required.

If these conditions exist, then I think there is reason to expect that an unknown number will choose to witness to their faith by publicly professing their desire to be poor, chaste, and obedient in imitation of Jesus Christ, reason to believe that the renewal of religious life will be both a model and an inspiration for the formation of alternative faith communities and for the ongoing reform of the church as a whole.

APPENDIX

Interview Guide

1. Did you like the food when you first entered?

2. Was any of it unfamiliar?

3. Could you eat as much as you wanted?

4. Could you refuse to eat what you did not like?

5. Were snacks permitted?

6. How did the Easter Sunday dinner differ from Good Friday's?

7. Did you ever eat outside the refectory? If so, why?

8. What were the names/authors of some books that were read aloud?

9. Describe the environment: refectory art or wall hangings; tables (material, placement); dishes; utensils; seat assignment; method of serving; table manners; clean-up procedures.

10. (SND) Please indicate if you took part in the following in the novitiate and how often you did so: prostration; kissing feet; asking prayers and kissing feet; kneeling out; begging; reciting acts of reparation; asking penance of the novice mistress at the end of the meal.

    (OP) How frequently did you participate in the following: kneeling at the refectory door; kissing the feet of the sisters; sitting at "little table?"

11. (SND) When there was recreation at meals were any topics forbidden? Any encouraged?

    (OP) Did you notice any similarities between chapel ritual and dining ritual? If so, please specify.

12. When were you introduced to refectory penances and how were they explained to you?

13. In your opinion, what was the purpose of all these special behaviors?

14. Did these become a meaningful part of your spirituality?

15. Did your founder initiate these practices?

16. Would you prefer to be observing them now?

17. Did you ever speak of them to other sisters?

18. Did you ever speak of them to your family?

19. In actual practice was the focus of your attention during a meal on your penance, your food, your neighbor, or the reading?

20. What authority(ies) could and did initiate changes?

NOTES

CHAPTER 1

1. This was the first time that the director of postulants was more than an assistant to the director of novices. Since more than thirty candidates were applying annually, two people were considered necessary for formation. In this new division of duties the postulant director gave her own instructions to the new members.

Currently the congregation's population from all five entrance years (1960–64) totals twenty-three: seven remain from 1960, one from 1961, six from 1962, four from 1963, five from 1964.

The questionnaire was administered in person to three sisters who entered in 1960, three from 1962, and four from 1964. (See Appendix for the questionnaire.)

2. The sample represents eight different entrance years between 1914 and 1925. Three of the ten sisters made European novitiates and consider themselves missionaries to California.

CHAPTER 2

1. Chapter delegates, provincials, and formation personnel I consulted in California, Connecticut, and Maryland provinces named Massachusetts as the most rigid in the interpretation and enforcement of Institute customs. Two of those interviewed from Massachusetts had been stationed abroad and both made that same observation of their province. All conjectured that large numbers were responsible for the regimentation of life there.

2. Those now members of Notre Dame from all who entered between 1960 and 1964 in California and Massachusetts total eighty-two. The sample represents three from 1960, two from 1961, two from 1962, two from 1963, one from 1964.

3. Four sisters from the California province and six from Massa-

chusetts were interviewed. The distribution of entrance years was as follows: 1914, two; 1916, one; 1921, one; 1922, two; 1923, one; 1924, two; 1925, one.

CHAPTER 3

1. In Rahner's opinion this translation of the Christian kerygma from Judaism to Hellenism constitutes the model for what is needed today, so that the church of Rome can become a church for the world.

2. Evagrius named eight vices (gluttony, fornication, avarice, sloth, anger, discouragement, vainglory, pride) which entered the mainstream of the church as the seven deadly sins.

3. Margaret Miles identified four types of asceticism: those articulated by Egyptian desert dwellers, by early monastic founders, by St. Augustine, and by St. Ignatius of Loyola. I found, however, that another type emerged in the thirteenth century. A product of theological speculation on purgatory and the potential merit of self-induced pain, it differed from its predecessors in that penance was undertaken for the sake of the suffering souls, not just for interior growth in virtue.

4. The Institutions of 1220 were stamped with his ideas but he did not give them their final written form (Hinnebusch 1966: 85).

CHAPTER 4

1. These events were carefully recorded by Francoise Blin de Bourdon, a task delegated to her by Julie Billiart, who was ordered by Father Varin to commit the history of the congregation to writing as it unfolded.

2. The bones of her foot had been so mangled by inept surgery that a doctor examining her exhumed body in 1888 testified that walking should have been impossible. He hesitated to identify the body as that of Julie Billiart on these grounds (Linscott: 6).

CHAPTER 5

1. Soon after the death of St. Dominic the role of the lay brothers, which was originally quite creative and open-ended, became restricted to manual labor and routine tasks. Even in the twentieth-century United States their constitutions assumed illiteracy as their condition and the "hidden life" as their domain (*Constitutions of the Order of Saint Dominic for the Use of Laybrothers* [Vaticana: Tipografia Poliglotta, 1934]).

2. In the course of time many women in the third order took a

vow of celibacy and wore a habit. Ecclesiastical authority considers such to be religious and therefore subject to their regulations (Hinnebusch 1965: 400; 1966: 974).

3. In 1245 Ratisbon was placed in the care of the first order by Pope Innocent IV. It remained so until 1836 when it reverted to diocesan jurisdiction (Kohler: 299).

4. The family roles are in a period of transition, it seems. The language used by the present master general names the relationship between the Dominican men and women as "brother and sister"; he is not "over" them but "with" them (address at Mission San Jose, June 19, 1984); but his assumption of leadership roles (offered to him) at the Divine Office and at table prayers spoke more clearly of a "head of the house." The sisters present saw no contradiction between their definition of his visit (social call) and their interactions. When asked why he presided if he had no authority to do so, members of the Mission San Jose community met the question with incredulous looks and consistent response, "Because he's the master general."

5. The interpretation of perpetual silence in the refectory varied among the provinces. Friars from the East Coast of the United States reported that in any given year prior to Vatican II there might have been conversation at meals on thirty or forty occasions, to celebrate liturgical feasts or to be hospitable to visitors. Such dispensations from the rule were intended by St. Dominic, they maintained, for whom all rules were guidelines in the service of charity and the apostolate. Yearlong silent meals were observed only in the novitiate house. Friars in California, however, had a different experience. Their provincial superiors kept perpetual silence every day, including Thanksgiving and Christmas, and forbade priors and local superiors from issuing any dispensations from it.

6. Sisters of Notre Dame de Namur in the United States, by contrast, associated alcohol with medicinal cure, not with festive celebration. They were often allowed a "hot toddy" if they had a cold, or were treated with a tonic called "Beef, Iron and Wine" if they were anemic.

CHAPTER 6

1. Both congregations had unwritten regulations on sneezing, for example. When a Dominican sneezed, she lifted up the lower end of the napkin that was tucked inside her collar so that it shielded her face; the other hand pressed the handkerchief over nose and mouth. When a Sister of Notre Dame sneezed, she turned her head as far as possible over her shoulder (at that angle the shape of the bonnet completely hid her face from view), then used her handkerchief to muffle the sound.

2. Edward T. Hall coined the word "proxemics" for the study of culturally created environments. He was particularly interested in assessing effects of messages encoded in spatial organization on the inhabitants (1959, 1963, 1966).

3. The center tables shown in the diagram were a temporary necessity for approximately a five-year period when entrance groups were very large. Respondents who mentioned the center tables took care to inform me that they were "out of place." Their presence and the fact that people were seated on two sides of a table was disconcerting to many.

4. She who ranked highest in any entrance group was given more responsibilities, e.g., she was in charge of the set in the mistress's absence. Those who reviewed the applications admitted that the date of application was not the only criteria for assigning rank.

5. In current catalogs, rank (not alphabet) orders the listings.

6. In the nineteenth century bishops reported to Rome that lay superiors (not trained in moral theology and unable to get that training) were frequently abusing the rights of subjects by forcing a manifestation of conscience, even in matters proper to the confessional, and in some cases not keeping the confidences thus received. Pope Leo XII in the Decree "Quemadmodum" (1890) forbade all superiors to induce such a manifestation, although it could be received, if freely offered. In Canon 530 (1917) religious subjects were not encouraged to manifest their doubts and anxieties of conscience to lay superiors; but, fully aware that Saints Benedict, Francis of Assisi, and Teresa of Avila were all lay superiors and wise directors of souls, the church did not absolutely forbid spontaneous manifestations (Dee 1960: 91; 1967: 162).

CHAPTER 7

1. In a survey of 437 congregations (commissioned by the Conference of Major Superiors of Women) 37 percent reported procedures for psychological screening in place in 1966; 63 percent had them in 1982 (Neal 1984).

EPILOGUE

1. Living "singly" refers to those sisters who are the only members of their congregation living with other religious or with laity.

2. Approximately 95 percent of the Dominicans are employed in formal education, as compared with 50 percent of Notre Dame (California).

3. The last mission house (residence) was opened in 1969.

BIBLIOGRAPHY

The archival material proper to each congregation is listed below in order of date of publication.

Books that were published by the sisters or intended chiefly for the sisters but which were available to the public are listed under general literature. If I located these books in congregational archives, I placed the word "archive" in brackets at the end of the citation. The locations of the archives and the names of the archivists are given in the Preface.

ARCHIVAL DOCUMENTS

DOMINICAN SISTERS, CONGREGATION OF THE QUEEN OF THE HOLY ROSARY, MISSION SAN JOSE, CALIFORNIA ARCHIVES

1876. Letter of December 5 to Mother Pia Backes from Reverend Michael May.

1903. Letter of August 21 to the membership from Mother Pia.

1910 (ca.). "Ceremonial of the Congregation of the Queen of the Most Holy Rosary of the Third Order of St. Dominic." Handwritten and duplicated.

1923, 1937, 1952. *The Rule of St. Augustine and the Constitutions of the Third Order of St. Dominic of the Congregation of the Queen of the Holy Rosary.*

1937, 1943, 1949, 1955, 1961, 1967, 1985. *Acts of the General Chapter of the Congregation of the Queen of the Holy Rosary* (Eighth through Thirteenth Chapters, Eighteenth Chapter). Mission San Jose, Calif.: By the Sisters.

1966. *Dominican Community Prayers.* St. Albert the Great Province: Provincial Liturgical Commission for the Dominican Interprovincial Liturgical Commission.

1967. *Necrology of 1961–1967.* Mission San Jose, Calif.: By the Dominican Sisters.

1973, 1984. "Constitutions and Statutes of the Dominican Sisters, Congregation of the Queen of the Holy Rosary."

1982. "Community Catalog, Dominican Sisters of the Congregation of the Queen of the Holy Rosary."

SISTERS OF NOTRE DAME DE NAMUR, BELMONT, CALIFORNIA, ARCHIVES

1891. *Catechism of the History of the Institute of the Sisters of Notre Dame.* Cincinnati: Notre Dame Press.

1893a. *Observance of Rules.* An address by an anonymous Jesuit retreat master to the Sisters of Notre Dame at the Summit. Cincinnati: Notre Dame Press.

1893b. *The Private Rules of the Sisters of Notre Dame (Drawn up by our dear and venerated Mother St. Joseph and left us in her own handwriting; to which is added her fundamental maxims for a Sister of Notre Dame).* Cincinnati: Notre Dame Press.

1934a. "Customs of the Sisters of Notre Dame." Typewritten.

1934b. *Little Treatise of Perfection for the Use of the Sisters of Notre Dame of Namur: Extracts from the Writings of Our Holy Foundresses Followed by the Directory.* London: Burns Oates and Washbourne.

1934c. "Recommendations." Typewritten.

1947. *Manual of Prayers for the Use of the Sisters of Notre Dame de Namur.* Waltham, Mass.: By the Sisters.

1948. *Customs and Recommendations of the Sisters of Notre Dame de Namur.* Waltham, Mass.: By the Sisters.

1951. "Decisions of the Sixth General Chapter." Typewritten.

1955. "Private Rules of the Sisters of Notre Dame de Namur." American revision. By the Sisters.

1957. "Directives of the Seventh General Chapter—for the Superiors."

1957. "Directives of the Seventh General Chapter—for the Sisters."

1963. "The Customs and Recommendations of the Sisters of Notre Dame de Namur." Compiled Jan. 1, 1966. Typewritten, edited to show articles in continuous use from the early twentieth century.

1963. "Directives of the Eighth General Chapter." Typewritten.

1969. *Acts of the Special General Chapter of the Sisters of Notre Dame.* Baltimore: Garamond/Pridemark.

1983. Letter of September 16 to author from Sister Marie Chantal, SNDN (Belgian Prov.).

1984a. Letter of October 1 to author from Sister Agnes Immaculata, SNDN.

1984b. *Constitutions and Directory.*

1984–87. Directories of Sisters of Notre Dame de Namur: Boston Province, California Province, Ipswich Province.

1986. "Internal Environment Study." Sisters of Notre Dame de Namur, California Province. Pamphlet.

SOCIETY OF JESUS, LOS GATOS, CALIFORNIA, ARCHIVES

1883. *Directions for the Novices of the Society of Jesus in California.* Santa Clara College: By the Members.

1960. "Custom Book of the American Assistancy of the Society of Jesus." For Ours only.

GENERAL LITERATURE

Abbott, Walter, SJ, ed. *The Documents of Vatican II.* New York: American Press, 1966.

Backes, Reverend Mother Pia, OP. *Her Days Unfolded.* Translated from the German by Mother Bernardina Michel, OP. St. Benedict, Ore.: Benedictine Press, 1953 [OP archives].

Baum, Gregory, OSA. "Commentary." *The Decree on the Renewal of Religious Life of Vatican Council II*, promulgated by Pope Paul VI on Oct. 28, 1965; translated by Austin Flannery. Glen Rock. N.J.: Paulist Press, 1966.

Baur, Francis, OFM. *Life in Abundance: A Contemporary Spirituality.* New Jersey: Paulist Press, 1983.

Belz, Carl. *The Story of Rock.* New York: Oxford University Press, 1972.

Bland, Joan. s.v. "Notre Dame de Namur, Sisters of." *New Catholic Encyclopedia*, vol. 10. New York: McGraw-Hill, 1967.

Brake, Michael. *Comparative Youth Culture: The Sociology of Youth Culture and Youth Subcultures in America, Britain, and Canada.* Boston: Routledge and Kegan Paul, 1985.

Brodrick, James, SJ. *Saint Ignatius Loyola: The Pilgrim Years 1491–1538.* New York: Farrar, Straus and Cudahy, 1956.

Brown, Rita Marie, OP. s.v. "Dominican Sisters of Mission San Jose, California." *New Catholic Encyclopedia*, vol. 4. New York: McGraw-Hill, 1967.

Butler, Christopher. *The Theology of Vatican II.* London: Darton, Longman and Todd, 1981.

Bynum, Caroline Walker. *Holy Feast and Holy Fast.* Berkeley: University of California Press, 1987.

Cada, Lawrence, SM, et al. *Shaping the Coming Age of Religious Life.* New York: Seabury, 1979.

Chadwick, Owen. *John Cassian.* Cambridge: Cambridge University Press, 1968.

——. *Western Asceticism.* Philadelphia: Westminster Press, 1958.

Chisholm, Julie de la Sainte Famille, SNDN. "History of the Rules and Constitutions of the Sisters of Notre Dame de Namur" (print), 1954. [SND archives]

Chittister, Joan, OSB, et al., eds. *Climb along the Cutting Edge: An Analysis of Change in Religious Life.* New York: Paulist Press, 1977.

Clare, James, SJ, ed. *The Life of Blessed Julie Billiart: Foundress of the Institute of Sisters of Notre Dame.* Written by an anonymous Sister of Notre Dame [Mary Xavier Partridge]. Some chapters translated from Rev. Père Clair's *Life of Julie Billiart.* London: Sands and Co. [SND archives]

Cormier, Rev. Hyacinth, OP, et al. *Guide, Counsellor and Friend.* Mission San Jose, Calif.: By the Dominican Sisters. [OP archives]

Crawford, Rev. Eugene J. *The Daughters of Dominic on Long Island.* New York: Benziger Bros. [OP archives]

Dalton, David. *James Dean: The Mutant King.* New York: St. Martin's Press.

Dee, Dacian, OFM, Cap. *The Manifestation of Conscience.* Canon Law Studies No. 410. Washington, D.C.: Catholic University of America Press.

——. s.v. "Manifestation of Conscience." *New Catholic Encyclopedia,* vol. 9. New York: McGraw-Hill, 1967.

Deseille, Placide. s.v. "Jeûne." In *Dictionnaire de Spiritualité: Ascetique et Mystique, Doctrine et Histoire,* vol. 8. Paris: Beauchesne, 1974.

DiIanni, Albert, SM. "Vocations and the Laicization of Religious Life." *America,* March 14, 1987, pp. 207–11.

Douglas, Mary. "Deciphering a Meal." *Daedalus* 101 (1972): 61–81.

——. *Natural Symbols.* New York: Vintage, 1973.

——. *Purity and Danger: An Analysis of Concepts of Pollution and Taboo.* Baltimore: Penguin, 1970.

Elias, Norbert. *The Civilizing Process: The History of Manners.* New York: Urizen Books, 1978.

Evennett, H. Outram. *The Spirit of the Counter-Reformation.* Based on lectures delivered in 1951. Edited with a postscript by John Bossy, 1966. Notre Dame: University of Notre Dame Press, 1970.

Foucault, Michel. *Discipline and Punish: The Birth of Prison.* Translated by Alan Sherican. New York: Pantheon, 1977.

——. *Power/Knowledge: Selected Interviews and Other Writings, 1972–77.* Edited by Colin Gordon. New York: Pantheon, 1980.

Gallagher, Catherine and Thomas Laqueur, eds. *The Making of the Modern Body: Sexuality and Society in the Nineteenth Century.* Berkeley: University of California Press, 1987.

Gannon, Thomas, SJ, and George Traub, SJ. *The Desert and the City.* London: Macmillan, 1969.

Ganss, George E., SJ. *Constitutions of the Society of Jesus.* By Ignatius of Loyola. Translated with an introduction and commentary by George E. Ganss. St. Louis: Institute of Jesuit Sources, 1970.

Geertz, Clifford. *The Interpretation of Cultures.* New York: Basic Books, 1973.

Godfrey, Mary, SNDN, et al., eds. *The Memoirs of Mother Frances Blin de Bourdon.* Translated with a biographical supplement by Sister Mary Godfrey, SNDN, et al. Westminster, Md.: Christian Classics, 1975.

Goody, Jack. "Against 'Ritual': Loosely Structured Thoughts on a Loosely Defined Topic." In *Secular Ritual,* edited by S. Moore and B. Myerhoff, pp. 25–35. Amsterdam: Van Gorcum, 1977.

Guralnick, Peter. *Lost Highway: Journey and Arrivals of American Musicians.* Boston: Godine, 1979.

Hall, Edward T. *The Hidden Dimension.* Garden City, N.Y.: Doubleday, 1966.

———. "Proxemics." *Current Anthropology* 9 (1968): 83–106.

———. *The Silent Language.* Garden City, N.Y.: Doubleday, 1959.

———. "A System for the Notation of Proxemic Behavior." *American Anthropologist* 65 (1963): 1003–26.

Hammontree, Patsy G. *Elvis Presley: A Bio-Bibliography.* Westport, Conn.: Greenwood Press, 1985.

Hinnebusch, William A., OP. *Dominican Spirituality: Principles and Practice.* Washington, D.C.: Thomist Press, 1965.

———. *The History of the Dominican Order: Origins and Growth to 1500.* Vol. 1. Staten Island: Alba House, 1966.

Jarrett, Bede, OP. *The Religious Life.* London: Burns Oates and Washbourne, 1939.

———, ed. *Lives of the Brethren of the Order of Preachers, 1206–1259,* London: Blackfriars, 1955.

Jedin, Hubert and John Dolan. *History of the Church.* Vol. 7. New York: Crossroads, 1980.

Jungmann, Josef, SJ. *The Early Liturgy: To the Time of Gregory the Great.* Translated by Francis Brunner, CSSR. Notre Dame, Ind.: University of Notre Dame Press, 1959.

Kloppenburg, Bonaventure, OFM. *The Ecclesiology of Vatican II.* Chicago: Franciscan Herald Press, 1974.

Kohler, Mary Hortense, OP. *Mother Benedicta Bauer.* Milwaukee: Bruce, 1937. [OP archives]

Knowles, David, OSB. *Christian Monasticism.* New York: McGraw-Hill Book Co., 1969.

——. *From Pachomius to Ignatius: A Study on the Constitutional History of Religious Orders.* Oxford: Clarendon Press, 1966.

Lachowski, James, s.v. "Asceticism (In the New Testament)." *New Catholic Encyclopedia,* vol. 1. New York, McGraw-Hill, 1967.

Le Goff, Jacques. *The Birth of Purgatory.* Chicago: University of Chicago Press, 1984.

Levi-Strauss, Claude. "The Culinary Triangle." *Partisan Review* 33 (1966): 586–95.

Linscott, Mary, SNDN. *To Heaven on Foot.* Glascow: Burns and Sons, 1969. [SND archives]

Longridge, W. H., SJ. *The Spiritual Exercises of Saint Ignatius of Loyola.* London: Roxburghe House, 1919.

Lowen, Alexander. *Pleasure.* New York: Penguin Books, 1975.

McLoughlin, William G. *Revivals, Awakenings, and Reform: An Essay on Religion and Social Change in America, 1607–1977.* Chicago: University of Chicago Press, 1978.

Maguire, Catherine, RSCJ. s.v. "Varin D'Ainville, Joseph Desire." *New Catholic Encyclopedia,* vol. 14. New York: McGraw-Hill, 1967.

Mehegan, Mary Paul, OP, ed. *Women of the Word: Dominican Sisters of Mission San Jose, 1876–1976.* Mission San Jose, Calif.: By the Sisters, 1976. [OP archives]

Meyers, Bertrande, DC. *Sisters for the Twenty-First Century.* New York: Sheed and Ward, 1965.

Miles, Margaret R. *Fullness of Life: Historical Foundations for a New Asceticism.* Philadelphia: Westminster Press, 1981.

Neal, Marie Augusta, SNDN. *Catholic Sisters in Transition: From the 1960s to the 1980s.* Wilmington, Del.: Michael Glazier, 1984.

O'Connor, Terrence R., SJ. s.v. "Asceticism (Early Christian)." *New Catholic Encyclopedia,* vol. 1. New York: McGraw-Hill, 1967.

Official Catholic Directory. New York: P. J. Kenedy and Sons, 1963.

Olin, John C., ed. *The Autobiography of St. Ignatius Loyola.* Translated by Joseph F. O'Callaghan. New York: Harper Torchbooks, 1974.

O'Neill, John. *Five Bodies: The Human Shape of Modern Society.* Ithaca: Cornell University Press, 1985.

Ortner, Sherry. "Is Female to Male as Nature Is to Culture?" In *Woman, Culture and Society,* edited by M. Rosaldo and L. Lamphere, pp. 67–87. Stanford: Stanford University Press, 1974.

——. *Sherpas through Their Rituals.* New York: Cambridge University Press, 1977.

Ortner, Sherry and Harriet Whitehead. *Sexual Meanings: The Cultural Construction of Gender and Sexuality.* Cambridge: Cambridge University Press, 1981.

Quasten, Johannes. *Music and Worship in Pagan and Christian Antiquity.* Translated by Boniface Ramsey, OP. Washington, D.C.: National Association of Pastoral Musicians, 1983.

Quinn, John [bishop of San Francisco], ed. "Pontifical Commission Report to United States Bishops: United States Religious Life and the Decline of Vocations." *Origins* 16 (1986): 467–70.

Rahner, Hugo, SJ, ed. *St. Ignatius Loyola: Letters to Women.* New York: Herder and Herder, 1960.

Rahner, Karl, SJ. *Concern for the Church: Theological Investigations XX.* Translated by Edward Quinn. New York: Crossroads, 1981.

Reeves, John-Baptist, OP. *The Dominicans.* Westminster: Blackfriars, 1959 [orig. 1929].

Refoulé, Francois, OP. s.v. "Evagrius Ponticus." In *New Catholic Encyclopedia*, vol. 5. New York: McGraw-Hill, 1967.

Rosner, Francis, SNDN and Lucy Tinsley, SNDN, eds. *The Letters of Saint Julie Billiart.* Vol. 1. Rome: Gregorian University Press, 1974. [SND archives]

Rouillard, Philippe. "From Human Meal to Christian Eucharist." In *Living Bread, Saving Cup*, edited by R. Kevin Seasoltz, pp. 126–57. Collegeville, Minn.: Liturgical Press, 1982.

Rousseau, Philip. *Ascetics, Authority, and the Church: In the Age of Jerome and Cassian.* Oxford: Oxford University Press, 1978.

Roy, Samuel. *Elvis: Prophet of Power.* Brookline, Mass.: Branden, 1985.

Schmemann, Alexander. *Great Lent.* New York: St. Vladimir's Seminary Press, 1974.

Schmitz, Philibert. s.v. "Chapitre des Coulpes." In *Dictionnaire de Spiritualité: Ascetique et Mystique, Doctrine et Histoire*, vol. 2. Paris: Beauchesne, 1953.

Segundo, Juan Luis, SJ. *Grace and the Human Condition.* Vol. 2. Translated by John Drury. Maryknoll, N.Y.: Orbis Books, 1973.

Suenens, Cardinal Leon Joseph. *The Nun in the World.* London: Burnes and Oates, 1961.

Turner, Bryan S. *The Body and Society.* New York: Basil Blackwell, 1984.

Turner, Victor. *Ritual Process.* Ithaca, N.Y.: Cornell University Press, 1969.

Vermeersch, Arthur, SJ. *Miles Christi Jesu: Meditations on the Summary of the Constitutions.* From the third French edition, revised according to the official text of the Twenty-Seventh General

Congregation. For the use of Ours only. El Paso, Tex.: Revista Catolica Press, 1951. [SJ archives]

Weiser, Francis X., SJ. *Handbook of Christian Feasts and Customs.* New York: Harcourt, Brace and World, 1958.

Wright, John H., SJ. *The Order of the Universe in the Theology of St. Thomas Aquinas.* Vol. 89. Series Facultatis Theologicae. [Rome]: Universitatis Gregorianae, 1957.

INDEX